THE ADULT STUDENT:

An Insider's Guide to Going

Back to School

By Dani Babb, Ph.D., MBA

THE ADULT STUDENT:

An Insider's Guide to Going Back to School

Dani Babb, Ph.D., MBA

Cover Design and Artwork by Harper Media

The Adult Student

Editing by Thomas Dellner

Editing and Formatting by Mary Anne Donovan

Mandevilla Press
Weston, CT 06883

Library of Congress Cataloguing-in-Publication data pending.

ISBN 978-1-62704-007-5

Table of Contents

Dedication

This book is dedicated to my daughter, Jordan Alexandra Babb, who challenges me every day to be a better person, to love more deeply, to work harder, to prioritize life -- and perhaps most importantly -- to know when it is time to stop and just play. My two year old daughter is demanding and willful, just like someone else I know all too well! She is teaching me a new way of living, one that involves complete trust and unselfish love. This book took a lot longer to write than any other book I have written, and Jordan, thank you for that from the bottom of my heart.

Foreword

When it comes to going back to school, there are often more questions than answers available to would-be students. Most students get their advice from parents, colleagues, and even friends, or they get it from admissions reps after clicking a colorful ad at the school that caught their attention at just the right time.

Rarely is there an opportunity to hear from a credible, reliable, and balanced source whose advice is offered purely for your benefit.

That's where this book comes in. Dani Babb has years of experience in teaching online and on ground, as well as in earning degrees in both models. She has a unique perspective on how going back to school can impact your work life, your social life, your family life, and even your love life.

The best thing you can do as you prepare to move forward with your higher education goals is to take advice from someone who has faced the challenges you are facing and has made the decisions you are weighing.

All of the important factors you must weigh in your decision making process are addressed in this book, including how to choose a reputable school and program, and how to separate a school's marketing materials (both in for-profit schools and non-profit schools) from reality, and then what to expect when you get into class – whever you decided to go.

Dani's personal stories, as well as her wit and humor, will keep you turning the pages and, more importantly, will help you remember the important considerations that will help you make the best possible choice in the pursuit of your goals.

As a dean and a professor myself, I can attest to the quality of Dani's sound advice, the thoughtful research that backs up her guidance, and her fresh perspective on the benefits of furthering your education. Dani was my masters and doctoral mentor years ago, and also helped me figure out where to go to school when the time came. I have never regretted my decision.

I recommend this book to anyone that is serious about taking the next step in personal development, academic growth, and professional advancement. On a personal note, I'm glad to finally have a place to point folks who are weighing a return to school. After you read it, you'll recommend it to your friends and family, too.

Bill Luton, PhD

Dean of Business at Allied Schools

Candidate for North Carolina State House

District 1

Acknowledgements

I wish to acknowledge my good, good friend, who I am quite sure wishes to remain unnamed so he stays out of Google... but you know who you are. You give me confidence when I lack it even if you don't mean to, and make me laugh when we spend time together. I enjoyed the way we came up with the title for the book, and everything you do to help me in small and big ways. You also helped me with some key components for this book – and life - and I will be forever grateful. I respect you so much and love you to death.

I wish to acknowledge Dr. Bill Luton, a good friend and ally, who provided a kick every now and again when I needed it and some great, sound advice as we proceeded. IAL my friend.

I acknowledge - with much respect - Tom Dellner, rescuer of women from flying insects, brilliant writer, good friend and terrific editor. I am sure you wanted to pull your hair out many times, Tom, when you read this manuscript, and I promise to help pay for transplants and therapy when the time comes. In fact, just reading this unedited acknowledgements page will probably freak you out. I'm sorry for that... and for the mean notes. ☺

To Dr. Bob - you have kept me sane (or less insane) on more occasions than I can count. Thanks for being such a dear friend while life threw what felt like insurmountable curve balls on more occasions than is remotely logical.

To Bob Diforio, who has patiently worked with me for years on all sorts of books, and is always encouraging and has my back. He also tells me when my ideas suck, and I am appreciative for his candid advice. We made a wise choice, Bob.

To Mary Anne Donovan who worked so hard on this manuscript to edit it and format it and provide her insight and critiques along the way, and did it all while managing to not make me feel like an idiot. Thank you so much!

Last but not certainly least.. to my friends and family who are supportive, loving, rightfully beat me up (metaphorically of course) along the way and ask me the same thing I ask myself - what's next? Zack, you best have your book out before my next one, you brilliant writer you! Time will tell. I love you guys! :)

About The Author

Dani Babb, PhD, MBA
Founder and President of The Babb Group
Author, Professor, Television
Commentator

If you have picked up this book, you may be well on your way to deciding whether or not to go back to school! Congratulations - you have taken the first step towards investing in yourself with something that no one can take away from you. A tool that will help you market yourself going forward, engage in a new career, advance in an existing one, start a business, change professions, model to your children that you value education (and yourself), build self-confidence and your own skill set and knowledge. Yes, as you can tell, I am a big fan of education. I have devoted my second post-Information Technology (IT) career to engaging with students and professors to guide them in their quest to make their goals and dreams become reality. The fact is, today many of us do not get to go to school at "traditional times", or may find that we need a degree to maintain our competitiveness or move up in our field. I earned one of my degrees in a traditional state school, another in a private evening program, and another online. I have been an on ground and online professor since the early 1990s during a career in IT and after, when education became my only career. My roots in online education go back to the beta version of Blackboard. I have published many books on education and business, and I share my wins and losses openly. I am forthright and candid in my approach to business and education, knowing that mentoring is useless without it. My company, The Babb Group, is an educational consulting company focusing on helping students and professors make informed decisions.

That is my goal with this book - that you will walk away and know clearly whether you can and should go to school now, how to pick whether to go to school in an online or on ground format, and where to attend. Hundreds of professors and students shared in the journey along the way and offered their input and critique, criticism and suggestions, most of which I incorporated into this book. I am a Professor of Economics for American Military University and teach as an adjunct at other schools, working with students from associates level programs to doctoral programs. I teach economics, technology, statistics, business, management, and other practical subjects. I earned my **Doctorate in 2004** and my MBA in 1999. I am an analyst and commentator for cable and local news channels - FoxNews, Fox Business, MSNBC, NBC, CNN, Bloomberg and others. My pledge is to offer a unique perspective to educate consumers and students on what is taking place in the market, and to offer a fresh look for people on Main Street where analysis really counts. All of the data in the world doesn't matter if we don't know what it means. This is my approach to educating consumers, and I hope you find this to be a useful approach in this book as well. I co-authored the first mainstream book about online education called *Make Money Teaching Online* with Dr. Jim Mirabella in 2006, and this book is a natural progression from the educator side into the student side.

On a personal note, I am a workaholic and love analyzing markets and data, studying biology and medicine for fun, memorizing statistics and playing with new gadgets - particularly those that baffle friends who come into my home and cannot figure out how to turn the lights on anymore (and need a secret code to do it, even better!). I would describe myself as an antiestablishmentarianist who enjoys challenging the status quo and doesn't do things "just because they've always been done that way." I love people and their unique personalities and goals; I love the thrill of life – of success - and all the ups and downs that go with it. I sure prefer the ups but learn the most from the downs! I enjoy political strategy, travel, working out, healthy banter, fashion, wit, a great belly laugh, and providing for my daughter - oh, and carbon fiber. :) That just might be an obsession.

I live in Southern California and New York City with my two year old daughter; a nice blend of fast-paced and chill - though I far prefer the Big Apple to the retirement state of California. I have been very fortunate to be able to travel around the world, and have had the opportunity to meet many amazing people. I have visited most states and many countries, and stay on the road as often as my daughter and career allow. Most of all, I am grateful for wonderful and loving friends and family and I am committed to the success of our clients and readers.

Please stay in touch, whether by email, or social media. We have a lot of groups out there to support you from your initial decision all the way through graduation and beyond.

I'd love to hear from you.

My best wishes in your new pursuits,

Dani

Twitter:	twitter.com/danibabb
Facebook:	facebook.com/drdanibabb
YouTube:	youtube.com/thebabbgroup
Website:	www.thebabbgroup.com

Introduction

If you are reading this book, you're probably considering going back to school as an adult. Maybe you've earned a bachelor's degree, and now you want to earn a professional or graduate degree and you aren't quite sure how to go about doing it. Or perhaps you, like so many others, didn't have the opportunity to go to college at the "socially normal" time - right after high school - and have decided that now is the time to pursue your bachelor's degree. Or maybe you have chosen to selflessly serve our nation by joining the armed forces, and now after retirement, (or even while still on active duty), you are contemplating earning a degree to help you advance in your professional life, post-military.

Another reason so many are going back to school today? To paraphrase former president

1

Bill Clinton, it's the economy, stupid. It's a well-known fact that when workers are laid off, one choice they often make is to take advantage of their unplanned downtime to further their education and, in the process, advance their ability to be hired in the rebounding economy (and hopefully their salaries, too). Going back to school also presents networking opportunities, whether we are in a recession or not. Many going back to school today are in between jobs or are anticipating being downsized and want to enroll while they still have tuition reimbursement benefits remaining, or as part of a downsizing package. Some have been looking to change fields altogether and find that a recession, or being laid off, is the right time to do it – a built in excuse, as it were. It was a catalyst for me years ago and I haven't regretted it (but can sure relate to the anxiety of being "right-sized")

Whatever the reason, the Internet has brought us more choices in education than ever before. Some of you may have read my book *Make Money Teaching Online*, co-authored with

Dr. Jim Mirabella. That book, published in 2006, was the first-ever book on how to earn a living as an online professor or adjunct instructor, and it still a staple in the marketplace today for online teachers. But there's an important topic that book did not address: what should students look for in an online school? It's a critical issue, and one that's becoming increasingly complex with students presented with more options than ever before.

This book isn't meant to replace *Make Money Teaching Online* or even supplement our thoughts on how to become a professor (we will leave that to the sequel!), but rather to take another look at the world of online education—from a professor's viewpoint, written for the benefit of the student. It's a manual to provide insight on everything from choosing the right school to what we professors really think about your work (which you may or may not want to know!) I'll also share with you what other educators are thinking, using data from anonymous surveys and gathered from brave souls willing to share their viewpoints, and what deans and department chairs think about everything from accreditation to education quality. And, since I was asked by many online students to cover what we are really asked to assess in the classroom, I will delve into that topic, as well. Many students from online and traditional institutions also shared their insights for this book and are quoted throughout.

Finally, throughout this book you will notice that a lot of different terms are used that mean the same thing. For example offline education is on ground, brick and mortar or traditional education. Basically it means going into a building, whether an office building/annex or a traditional classroom, and learning from a person face to face. Online education is simply "online" throughout. Hybrid education is where most of your courses and your degree are from an on ground institution, but you may take a course or elements of a class (such as assignment submissions) in an online format instead.

Prologue

HIGHER EDUCATION: A LOVE STORY

I believe with any literature or book we read, it is important to know the point of view from which the writer is coming. To help you understand my viewpoint (and therefore biases, which I'll clearly and honestly disclose), let me share a bit about my background: I began my education in 1993 in what would be considered "traditional academia," enrolling at the University of California at Riverside. I graduated in 1997 with a Bachelor of Science in Business.

While completing my degree, I had taken a job as the Information Technology Director at Loma Linda University School of Public Health. Two weeks after graduating, I started work on my Master of Business Administration (MBA) at the University of Redlands, Whitehead College, a nighttime MBA program for working adults. I

5

then began working for Loma Linda University School of Allied Health as a part time course developer and nighttime instructor after my "day job" for the program's first graduating class in Health Information Management. I was teaching and working full time as an IT Director during my MBA program. I use separate terms "teaching" and "working." Why? Teaching never really felt like work to me. It was fun, and, as a bonus, I got paid for it.

After seven years at Loma Linda, I abandoned ship (from my IT job) and headed west leaving behind Southern California's smoggy Inland Empire (commonly and derisively referred to in California as "the 909") for Orange County where I worked for a DVD and multimedia company, IPC Communications, as Manager and later, Regional Director, of IT. I still made the commute once or twice weekly to Loma Linda to teach night courses until I did not want to make the drive anymore. I stopped teaching then, but I missed it. I dove head-first into my full-time career in IT and learned from a terrific Chief Information Officer about leadership, management, education and teaming. It was a vital experience that I am grateful for (so thanks Mike Wilson!).

RIGHT-SIZED, DOWN-SIZED AND CORPORATE AMERICA

As time would eventually tell me (again and again), I wasn't a great fit for Corporate America. First, I didn't much like people telling me what to do on a day–to-day basis, or more accurately, how to do it. This sounds spoiled; I don't mean it in the bratty sense although being a young professional I am not quite sure I made myself clear. I have severe insomnia (since the age of five), and having a random person (okay, a boss) tell me to be to work by 8:00 in the morning for a meeting that I felt wasn't a good use of my time, after sleeping just two hours, was just not a positive thing in my book. I relished the days at Loma Linda where I was held accountable for student achievement and outcomes instead of what time I punched in. I'd eventually "train" my bosses in new positions to count on me for objectives, but it was time consuming and resulted in a lot of sleepless nights.

At IPC, I was able to accurately assess what my skillset was—and was not. I was a damn good team leader; this was definitely my strength. I managed a regional and then global team, and made IT a profit center – the only profit center – for that division of the company. Soon the company closed its doors, keeping only our Michigan office open. Having spent two crippling winters in St. Joseph, Michigan and learning first-hand what "lake effect" really meant (it is not pleasant to a California girl), I didn't exactly yearn to relocate there full time as the CEO asked me to do. For the first two weeks, I didn't even know what that "scrubber" was in the back of the rental car – turns out it would have helped with that pesky ice-on-windshield problem. I turned down the offer to move, found all but five of my California team members jobs (I love helping people position themselves for a career, and now help professors make the transition into being a professor), and then found my own way to my next position for a home builder in the same area, also in IT.

I bought my first home around this time; I was 24 and feeling pretty good. But, I missed teaching. I missed the inherent flexibility in academia, but I also missed knowing that a person left my office with more knowledge than when he or
she arrived and that it was mutual – I learned a heck of a lot from my students. It was awkward being such a young professor, but it was relatively amusing to take a seat in the back row on day one of class and listen to all the students ask where the professor was, and then sit back in shock (and maybe horror) as I got up to begin going through our syllabus.

While I was working at the home builder (Standard Pacific), my role grew tremendously. I began computer system integrations nationwide that were vital to the growth of the business during the height of the real estate boom. I learned a lot about the markets then and definitely learned from the school of hard knocks in some painful ways.

At one point, while sitting on a flight home after spending over 40 weeks that year on the road, I was informed that when I returned I had to "right size" most of my team, who were on the road with me. This was precisely why Corporate America and I just did not get along. I realized I wanted (or needed) to go back to school to earn my doctorate (not for teaching purposes, but just because there was one more level I hadn't attained yet) yet my work schedule made it impossible to do a traditional program. I felt trapped between the future and the present and was not happy with the way our company was treating people. I wanted to be back in education again.

By now, the Internet was far more common than it was when I earned my other two degrees, or to date myself now (as I am no longer the tender age of 24), when my friends and I would destroy planets in Trade Wars on a BBS using our 300 baud modems. I searched online and heard about Capella University. I researched its quality, read about its regional accreditation, and asked around. I applied, was accepted and started with three classes. I knew I wanted to teach while I went to school but could not make the commute back to Loma Linda again.

During my doctoral program, I began applying for teaching jobs at other online universities, wondering if they would accept me without a completed doctorate. I had set up the first Blackboard Beta system at Loma Linda, which is the most popular learning management system or courseroom management system in the country, so I had some familiarity with online learning before it grew in popularity. I landed a couple of online teaching jobs, and taught on the side for fun. This time, though, there was no need to hide in the back row.

I found ways to handle the workload, like downloading all student assignments before a flight and hammering out work while flying, then uploading them when I landed. See kids, in those days our planes did not have internet access! I could read as fast as I typed (I refer to it as marginally fast, but I have had flight attendants and fellow airline passengers stop and stare, wondering if I am typing real words, so my friends urged me to say "lightning fast"). I attended my doctoral residencies, learned how to do research as quickly as I could, changed jobs (again), and went to work for another real estate company.

After just a few months, a new director came in above me, and told me that "no woman working for me will have an <insert expletive> PhD." That was when I knew I had to quickly get all of the tuition money I could from this company and work as fast as possible to get my degree, because he'd find a reason to remove me (and he did in a layoff). My husband at the time didn't want me to earn another degree either, because I would "have more degrees than he has". (Can you say, loser?)

I was newly single and incredibly determined, but scared, intimidated and anxious, three feelings many of you may have come to know very well, too.

Not quite earning enough from online teaching to pay the bills, I had to find yet another IT job. In 2004 I went to work for a commercial real estate company in Newport Beach. My boss was wonderful, and allowed me to do school work (and even teach) from the office as long as our company work got done. I finished my doctorate just a couple of months after beginning work there, and was teaching a few courses too. Within a year, the income from my "side job" of teaching surpassed that of my day job, and I left Corporate America—and the 8:00 a.m. meetings that I didn't want to attend—for good. I finally got to help people achieve their dreams and pay my bills at the same time.

Although I love every facet of education, my love affair with online teaching started in the '90s at Loma Linda, but it has been fueled by the incredible people I have met while working online. Many are now great friends; in fact when I count my close friends, I'd guess 95 percent of them were or are online colleagues. I live in a virtual cave; in 2011, I emerged briefly to work on ground for one online school just so I could "see humans." (This also ended badly – yet another reminder that I do not belong in Corporate America, punching a clock or reporting to insecure or incompetent people!). After that stint, I refocused my work on my business, growing The Babb Group, helping educators and students, and applying what I have learned in and out of Corporate America to books and my clients. I am grateful to have had a chance to refocus and do the thing I love the most.

In 2010, I had another unexpected life event – a pregnancy that began in January of 2010 and resulted in eight months of bed rest. I won't bore you with the incredible details and statistical odds of the complications of that pregnancy in this book, but it is "Google-able" if you are curious. In June of 2010, I was admitted into the hospital, not to be released until the end of August after giving birth to my daughter, Jordan Alexandra. She was in the NICU for five weeks, and is sitting here beside me on a New York City-bound American Airlines flight, as I write the beginning of this book—it's her ninth cross-country flight since she was born. She has more frequent flyer miles than my parents have accumulated in ten years. I wear that as a badge of honor on her behalf until she's old enough to know how cool it is.

While other women were staring at the ceiling, counting tiles in the ante-partum and not knowing how to pass the time we were "incarcerated," I was holding dissertation defense calls for my learners, graduating doctoral students and grading papers for 18 hours a day —quite literally. My office manager came to Hotel Hoag (the name of the hospital was Hoag, and to make it feel less awful, I referred to it as a Hotel) every two days to discuss business, get outgoing mail, bring documents and handle my company activities, and my room was completely set up with full access to the Internet. I convinced a few hospital staffers to go back to school and taught nurses on the night shift about molecular biology when I could not sleep. New doctors, or those covering for others, were fuming mad that I was "working while on bed rest"; however, most soon realized that work didn't stress me out; *not* working stressed me out. The sign on my door "Private, Keep Out" was a running joke between my new nurse-friends – it meant I was sleeping or working and was not open to physician visits unless it was an emergency.

During this entire ordeal, and my nearly three month hospitalization over eight months, a few things kept me sane: my laptop, my ability to find some sense of control in the uncontrollable, writing a case study about the medical conditions which plagued my daughter and me, my renewed sense that there was something bigger and more important in life than the things I took for granted, knowing I would soon get to see my daughter, knowing I had the best doctors, my students, my bosses (did I just say that?!), my online and "on ground" friends, and knowing I was still "providing" for my new family. As a soon to be single parent, , I needed all of the income I could get to support us. This only further grew my love affair with online education.

I worked every day in the hospital, including the day of my surgery to get a few quick posts in before the anesthesia hit. I had some help from good friends' right after Jordan was born, but mostly I took care of business. I stayed four more days in the hospital and found a way to spring myself loose despite the doctors' strong recommendations to the contrary. I returned to the hospital NICU twice each day to take care of my little girl the only way I could, holding her while she was hooked up to a morass of wires and tubes and doing much of the clinical work myself (another passion). I often brought my laptop there, too, and worked out of the family waiting room so I could hold her whenever she woke up.

Work kept me sane. In no other job could I have done this but online teaching. My goal was having students not even realize I was in the hospital, and to this day most do not know.

REAL BONDS IN AN ONLINE ENVIRONMENT

During my time in Hotel Hoag, I grew a greater appreciation for the bonds you can and do create in the online world. After I regained my health, I became even more driven to help people get into online education – as students and professors. I started a mentoring business to help others become educators, and started a job-lead service to help professors find additional teaching jobs. Shortly after, I started writing this book.

I have to say upfront that I am a big advocate of online education, even though two-thirds of my degrees are from brick and mortar institutions. I realize online education isn't a good fit for everyone, so one of my goals with this book is to help prospective students determine if it is or isn't the right choice for them. I will weigh the pros and cons of both choices so you can make one that makes the most sense for you and your family.

So what's the point? The point is I have a ton of experience—my good friends joke that I live in dog years and that, in actuality, I am really 200-plus years old – thank God for ***botox***.–I have been around the proverbial block—in the corporate world, with health issues, amid suffering and stress, and in education. I have been hired, fired, rehired, refired and downsized in education and in the business world. I know what professors say and what they are thinking (well the ones willing to share!) I know what students should look for in an educational institution and how different factors may impact their ability to be successful. I enjoy cutting through the nonsense in marketing flyers and getting to the brass tacks so students are not ripped off. I have no problem telling others my viewpoint in a (hopefully) constructive manner. I have a view of traditional academia and online academia, how they differ and how they are similar. I have experience in for-profit education and not-for-profit education—another vital distinction you will want to keep in mind when deciding where to go to school.

With that, I write this book—for those of you wondering how to navigate the world of education today, how to find a school that will help you build your resume, and what the heck to make of the nasty rumors and emerging legislation circling the for-profit education sector. I have worked and do work in for-profit education, not-for-profit education, state schools, private schools, faith-based schools, anti-faith-based schools (yes, I have run into one that fired me abruptly after appearing on Hannity – ah, the war stories) and everything in between. I have taught hybrid courses (partly on ground and partly online) and fully online courses. I've worked on ground for an online school. In short, I have had the pleasure of working with thousands of students in my 15 years in education, from associate-level learners to learners earning a second (even third) doctorate.

In this book, I share all I can to help you make wise decisions. And perhaps more important, I've included questions and answers with students and other education experts so you get a more rounded, less biased view of the world of higher education in today's market.

Enjoy, and happy learning!

Chapter 1: Traditional or Online Education: Which is Right for You?

You have more choices in education today than any other time in history. If you are thinking of going back to school, you can select an on ground traditional college, an on ground evening or adult program, a hybrid university combining online and on ground elements, or a fully online school. Once that choice is made, you have many others to follow, including: how to decide which school is right for you? Which program is the best for career advancement? How is for-profit education viewed by hiring managers? What qualities in education matter most to you? Of course in addition to those are numerous other personal decisions you must make. In this first chapter, I'll introduce the high level options and some of the benefits and drawbacks to both online and on ground options. So as to not waste time, I'll get right into it!

Online Education

Online education is becoming incredibly popular in today's market. An increasing number of students are enrolling in online educational programs—whether they are offered by brick-and-mortar institutions or fully online, for-profit schools—to earn a degree. There are millions of students going to school online and that number is growing considerably. Online courses are even popping up at some of the most prestigious, traditional schools like Harvard and Yale (although I can assure you that many of the professors and graduates look down on online education) and many state schools like Arizona State University. Nearly 10 percent of students today pick one of the 500 for-profit schools in the United States to earn their degree, and most of these students are adults. In fact, it is estimated that almost 80 percent of students will have taken at least one online course by the time they graduate.

In the prologue, I confessed a bit of a bias toward online education. Here's why: it's flexible, and many of the professors you will have in your online programs first taught in traditional schools (which makes the argument that the professors in online education are not as high of quality utterly illogical). Online schools have been around long enough that they have dealt with many of the issues they had with quality and reputation. Initially, some unethical schools, motivated by greed, gave the entire sector a bad reputation. That isn't to say some problems aren't serious, but they are far less prevalent today than they were five years ago. Online students today have to engage in thorough, online graded discussions (are your discussions in on ground courses graded?). If a student earns a scholarly doctorate online, she has to do the same dissertation research that any student in any program has to do. In my own doctoral program, I had 10 comprehensive exam questions (now the school has three), three residential on ground weeks on research, and a dissertation committee of three (plus the usual school reviews).

Offline Education

I have taught in two on ground evening or adult education programs. I taught at the highly reputable Chapman College in California, and for the already mentioned Loma Linda University, also in California. Yes, you will get peer-to-peer and instructor-to-peer interaction. Is it more interaction than you might get online? From my perspective, absolutely not – it is just different. I was one of the professors who hung out after class to talk with students for an hour or two about their careers, questions they had about course material, and the dozens of other things traditional students want to talk about. Usually one to three students in every class like to keep you until 11:00 p.m. when the security guard finally knocks on the door. However, in online education, it is just the vehicle that changes. My students use email or instant messenger instead, but they still have my attention and they have it seven days per week, as opposed to one night per week. In fact, they have more of it as I check email throughout the night.

My experience in continuing education programs was at the University of California at Irvine, where I taught courses online about buying and investing in real estate and becoming an online teacher. Many of my colleagues have taught in on ground continuing education programs and liken them to the online evening degree-based programs. Every survey I have I conducted shows similar responses to evening degree-based programs in terms of instructor commitment and student time required for course completion. Just because you are taking a course on ground does not necessarily mean that your professor will be any more available for you. In fact, you may have to work around very strict office hours without the luxury of emailing or texting your professor.

There are also additional costs that we do not always factor in, like the cost of transportation, of meals, of the time and cost to commute, issues finding parking (and of course the cost of the permit) and needing to drag yourself into an on ground course when you are sick or someone in your family is and needs you around. If you have group work, chances are your group will want to meet on ground and not virtually, which also adds time and costs. There are of course benefits to these things too; the added camaraderie, the benefit of really getting to know someone in person, and the networking possibilities.

What the Numbers Say

In reality, there is no such thing as pure offline education anymore. There are now digital textbooks, online learning management systems, the availability of online courses within a traditional degree program: even the Ivy League schools are offering some online courses now.

The quality of higher education is a matter of great concern to all future adult students and that means YOU! In a study done in 2011 by the

PEW Research Center, 2,142 adults were asked if they thought online education was of the same quality as offline education. Interestingly, 29 percent of the respondents said no, it was not. Then, the same year, a survey was conducted of 1,055 college presidents asking the same question and the result was that 51 percent felt the quality of online education was just as good as traditional education.

Now let's look at something else. Among students who have graduated from traditional schools in the last 10 years, 46 percent have taken an online course. Also, adult students who have taken an online course say the quality is just as good as an in-classroom course.

What Students and Professors Say

In the section that follows I identify some of the pros and cons of online and offline higher education and let you know what others say, too.

A CASE FOR ONLINE EDUCATION

There are many advantages to online education. In my opinion (and in the opinions of the more-than 150 colleagues I interviewed for this book); the most important are:

Flexibility   You can work when you want to. If you are a night owl like me, you may find you work best long after others are in bed. Good luck doing that from 5:30 until 10:00 p.m. in your MBA on ground cohort. If you are juggling family and/or work obligations, flexibility becomes even more vital to your ability to achieve success. I teach many students in the military serving overseas that are still enrolled in school full time.

Adaptability   As life changes (including moves across the country, or to another country!) your education can adapt with you, too. You can be living in India and taking your courses just the same as you would in St. Louis. If you need to move for a job in this uncertain economy, you can do so without disrupting your program or needing to transfer units and start over at a new school. Online education is adaptable to what is going on in your life.

Prestige

Online schools have come a long (very long) way since their inception. But most would argue that despite their strength, they are not Ivy League quality. If the name on your diploma matters a great deal to you but you need to attend school in a flexible environment, consider a hybrid program with a more traditional school that has an online element. My degree from Capella isn't disregarded by anyone I'm aware of, but it isn't Harvard.

Transferability

In education, when it comes to transferability, it's all about accreditation. I address this in more detail later, but if you choose an accredited program, you can transfer units in (or out) the same as you could in traditional education.

Networks

This can be an upside or a downside depending on your personal style, also something I will discuss later in this chapter. If you are an introverted person, you may find yourself participating more in an online class. Just for kicks, I did an unofficial study of those participating on ground and online in one of my hybrid courses. When we were in class, the shy students didn't speak up. In the online format, those same students were more likely to throw their hat into the ring and comment on the various topics in class – they even engaged in vigorous debates with some of their classmates!

Some argue that you can't network well online; I argue the opposite. My strongest networks have been online, but I am a writer by default. This isn't always a good fit for some learning styles. When I give speeches, I often throw in some comment that I think will be funny only to see the audience stare at me with blank faces (ugh). While this occurs (and you may have been doing this already reading my work!), at least I don't know it's happening when I'm online, which makes me more apt to be myself and to share anyway. The same thing happens as a student. So yes, you can network online; for some of us, we network better or more easily online because we write in a more passionate way than we speak. Social media certainly helps this ability to connect with online alumni groups. However, for those schools lacking official communication tools for students may have faculty, like me, who create unofficial groups and count on word of mouth among students to share information.

You can have a life!

Yes, it's an advantage to online education. This in no way means it is less demanding. Many of my students (and 82 percent of respondents in a poll I conducted for this book) who took one degree on ground and one online said the online program was more demanding of time, thought and writing skill than their on ground courses. This is also an advantage, because so many employers want technically savvy people to work for them. You can gain this tech savvy and still tuck your kids in at night instead of missing dinner and bed time.

Rigor

Yes, this should be considered a benefit! Rigor in online academia as schools try to maintain (or for some, acquire) a positive image means they will grade nearly everything, from your discussion posts (including word-countto your ability to synthesize information. In traditional education, chatting about coursework usually isn't graded, even if your attendance might be. Some find this type of "writing rigor" too demanding but I rarely hear someone say "wow, getting an online degree sure was easy."

A CASE FOR ON GROUND EDUCATION

If you Google "for-profit online education," you will probably find many reports about scandalous behavior, unethical recruitment practices and downright lies to customers (students) that are so unethical they are nauseating. This represents a small number of schools, and even many of these cleaned up their act pretty fast (or were put out of business). As frustrating as the reports were for schools that weren't violating rules to be lumped in with those that were, the allegations really did provide more structure and integrity in the institutions.

Here are some valid concerns about online education that might encourage you to opt for an on ground program.

Concerns About Longevity	While I don't think this is an issue, some argue that online schools might not be around forever and that the degree will be

worth nothing if (or when) the school folds. Admittedly I worried about this with Capella a little bit in the old days. I have zero worries now. My first thought was that "it's too big to fail" now, but we know as with banks, there is no such thing. Reputation matters and Capella has a good one. So selecting an institution with a good reputation, even if it's more expensive, is vital.

Reputation

The reputation of online colleges isn't always favorable and I have met many traditional academics who would like to see online education banished for good. Some would argue that, in general, the reputation of online schools is unfavorable. In fact, even on the Yahoo Groups that I run and manage (you can sign up for them for free on my website at www.thebabbgroup.com) some of the online professors don't speak highly of online schools! I repeat, these are the professors!

35

You have a few options on how to handle this. You can find a reputable fully online school, or you can go with an on ground school that has an online option. You will get the reputation and name on your diploma of the on ground school, but the flexibility of the online school. Check state schools, community colleges and most traditional academic institutions to see if they offer a fully (or mostly) online program.

Prestige

Online schools have come a long (very long) way since their inception. But most would argue that despite their strength, they are not Ivy League quality. If the name on your diploma matters a great deal to you but you need to attend school in a flexible environment, consider a hybrid program with a more traditional school that has an online element. My degree from Capella isn't disregarded by anyone I'm aware of, but it isn't Harvard.

Traditional Networks

If you went to a school like University of Southern California and have had the experience of walking into an interview, having the manager realize you are fellow alum and hiring you nearly on the spot, you may not be happy with the networking opportunities of online education. We are spread out all over the world; students come from all over. It's rare you'll find a fellow alum from your program living in the same city, let alone someone you went to class with every day who would then hire you later, unless you want to be an online professor! Social media has helped the ability to network after you graduate quite a bit however.

Alumni Associations

The alumni associations at online schools, if they exist at all, leave much to be desired. If you are looking for an alumni association run the way they are in traditional academia, you will be sorely disappointed. Some schools send out newsletters or email campaigns to alum or hold networking events but more than that is wishful thinking.

Social Events

In short, there really aren't any, unless WebEx is your idea of a good time. There aren't events, parties or anything remotely resembling such in the online world. While I personally consider this a benefit as we can get a lot more done, many consider it a big downside. A social event might consist of a get-together at a residency if your school has that requirement, but beyond that, don't look for your online school to spark your social life or help you get your Mrs. Degree, as my mother used to say.

What Professors and Students Are Saying

"Online education offers increased exposure to diverse viewpoints. In an on ground classroom, you typically do not see a single mother from Dallas, a retired laborer from Portland, a laid-off auto-worker from Detroit, sitting alongside traditional and international students. Online classrooms offer more diverse perspectives, and thereby greater learning opportunities, for and from students of multiple national, ethnic, racial, geographic, socio-economic, and generational backgrounds."

~~~~~

Brent Ferns

"Review your program requirements; take time to find out if there are certain classes offered only certain

39

times of the year, in order to arrange your classes so there is no last minute fire alarms.... some schools, you have a personal adviser that can be relied on to give you this information (like Capella, where I received my MS); others, that is not the case (like Walden, where I am pursuing my PhD). Also, networking is highly beneficial - you may or may not be academically isolated doing your degree online, but meeting other students is socially and psychologically 'good medicine'. It may even help your career. Some of us are better networkers than others - if you do residencies, try to use some of your energy to connect with others in your field - then connect with them on LinkedIn."

~~~~~

Debra Yvonne Mathis

"Having access to all materials, lectures are delivered in written or video format and can be re-read and re-read, a video can be watched and watched. In a classroom if a student misses a class or doesn't write down an important fact, it is possibly gone. But in the online classroom, the student can go back over materials until mastery is reached. Certainly the flexibility of time for the student [can be a benefit]. The student can work or "attend" class anytime without driving, parking, etc. But there is also not the time constraint of a 50 minute class; professors can explain concepts, answer questions until understanding is gained. A bell does not stop engagement."

~~~~~

Dr. Sue Kavli

"Brent I also found that students in the on-line class were more open to offering points in a discussion because they did not have the fear of instant rejection from classmates or the instructor. They could also use more time to think through their responses and usually offered more to the conversation. Drawback was that I sometimes had to "mandate" they participate in the discussion."

~~~~~

Patrick Mattson

"Agree with all of the great comments above. Add that online students can gain experience working with a broader range of professors. Like students, online professors can teach from anywhere. Wouldn't it be great if a student could be mentored from professors all over the country and even the

world? Especially when it comes time to leave academics?"

~~~~~

Phil Hillard

"I'd argue perseverance. When you go to a traditional school you have access to resources that are unavailable via online learning. In a virtual environment you are it. It's important to remember - you can do this. You have to decide that you want it."

~~~~~

Frank Clay

"I think it creates an environment where people feel less inhibited in participating. Maybe there's a word for that which I am lacking at the moment, but basically, it allows students to speak up and get involved

43

in their classes without fear that everyone is looking at them or that they will be ridiculed in person. I think it makes it easier for the shy person to interact."

~~~~~

Karen Warburton

"I agree. Online discussion forums remove what I call "the shyness factor". Additionally, the asynchronous nature of discussion forums in online classrooms allows students to ponder an asked question and take the time to think critically before answering the initial question and responding to fellow students. In-class discussions often move so fast that students don't have time to show critical thinking skills. Do you

guys remember driving home from class and thinking, 'Oh. I should have said...'?" He continues, "Dani I found that my students retained the information longer and with better recall when they used the interactive agents that I deployed (heavy use of simulation). They became active participants (not all liked this at first) and at the end many told me it was one of their better learning experiences. I took on-line graduate classes in Online Teaching and Instructional Design after I had taught in a collegiate classroom for over 20 years and was amazed at how much I learned. The student controls (within limits) when and where they choose to learn/attend class; they are not time nor place bound. This helps those night owls who do not do well at those nasty

0800 classes. And allows the early birds to study at 0530 or so; each scenario better suits the students' internal clock."

~~~~~

Patrick Mattson (again, as he says)

"Also the ability to find a field of study that meets your needs; as a working professional, you aren't limited to what is offered at a university in your area."

~~~~~

Pamela Barden

"More involvement in discussions between classmates and the instructor. Better writing skills. Learning how to be a better communicator."

~~~~~

Michelle Worley

"Diversity and Culture: Online schools attract a wide range of students, many working in their home countries. Learning practical applications on an international scale direct from peers is an invaluable experience. Online schools also offer the ability to have teachers/professors/mentors from various places. I'm currently taking courses from mentors in Australia, New York and India. Their personal experience in a global setting cannot be matched in a classroom setting. Finally what we as students bring to a course. We bring our own dynamic, our own experience and our own background to the course and that creates life time experience."

~~~~~

Craig Eisenbrown

On Ground Education

On ground education has a rich history in the world. It is generally considered the benchmark for higher education, the standard upon which the others – including for profit education – based themselves, at least in the early days. On ground education has many benefits for those of you returning back to school.

If you are attending a prestigious university, you are likely to meet professors and peers (fellow students) who are high caliber individuals with rich professional lives and experiences. While many of your online classmates will also, sometimes it is tough to tell from a paragraph-long biography in the beginning of class and even harder to really get to know someone and network with them. You may meet professors who are well known in their fields, and while they also exist online, many of the infamous professors still work at brick and mortar institutions. Statistically you are likely to find older professors with more years of wisdom behind them at a brick and mortar college.

If you are a very social person, you may enjoy the camaraderie and the ability to make lifelong friends in your on ground program which can be difficult to get in an online course. In the evening MBA program that I was a part of, we created a Yahoo group for ourselves and we stay in contact through Facebook. Most of us remember the personalities and unique character traits of one another, and there is a nostalgia associated with the memories. I remember Marcia, the woman of few words, a crazy lady whose name I cannot remember (but I remember how crazy she was), the "two Jims", Wanda and Kent who were holding down full time jobs and full time family life while going to school together, Jake who presented a lot about his company with zest, and many others. I know that if I needed a job in Information Technology, they would take my call.

There is also something comforting to some people about the structure behind on ground or traditional education. You have class at a specific time, assignments due on specific dates, and if participation is mandatory or results in earned points, you generally just need to show up and not write pages and pages into a discussion forum. Sometimes it is easier to work in groups when the folks in the class live close to one another instead of trying to adjust to time zones and work virtually. At the end of the program, you will likely have a solid group of friends and peers for life.

Chapter 2: A Media Firestorm: Recent Issues in Online Education

Online education colleges that are for-profit have been under heavy fire by legislators, the media, those in traditional education and Ivy Leaguers for years. But in 2010, several things happened that caused a firestorm.

Why the Bad Rap?

When I was a small child, I remember going to my dad's Oroweat® depot where his team loaded bread at one in the morning to deliver to local grocers. There was a sign on the wall above the administrative area that read, "One bad apple can ruin the whole bunch." It had a vivid image of an apple spoiled in the middle of a basket, an image that obviously stuck in my memory. Many of us believe this is what happened in online education; the reputation of many was tarnished by the poor oversight and greed of a few.

While states were busy allowing K-12 education to go online with 2010-2011 being the busiest "approval" years for such advancement, online higher education schools were still instituting new policies and practices to fight regulators and to prove to accrediting agencies and the Department of Education that they were providing quality instruction that leads to positive outcomes. The result of this for professors has been astounding; much more oversight, micro management and policies that are so intense many have left the profession or went back to their day jobs. However, for students it has mostly been positive, as the new structures have helped ensure quality, timeliness, and oversight for your education and investment.

Legislation

Most of the legislation and regulation that the government has mandated—or is attempting to mandate— primarily affects the for-profit education sector. As those of us in business know, when a company aspires to earn a profit, it will need to offer some competitive advantage. For those that choose quality online, for-profit education, they get the benefit of a company that is in the business of education, competing with others, which tends to improve the choices, opportunities and overall quality for consumers (or in this case, students). However others argue that profit has no place in education, and that education should not be a business because it misrepresents its benefits and costs to consumers. My own online alma mater has done a great job keeping the reputation of the school up – not only because it's the right thing to do and deserves it – but because it is a for-profit company and they need to increase shareholder value. Personally, I am grateful that the invisible hand is also helping ot maintain the value of my degree. You may not be however and need to seriously consider that when you are deciding where to go to school.

It is important to note that you can certainly go to school in an online format at a not-for-profit university. But this area—governmental regulation of online education—is so conceptually difficult to understand, I think it is important to provide some background information, explain what has happened so far and discuss the implications for you as a potential student.

Online education has received more press and public scrutiny in the last two years than at any other time. The Department of Education (DOE) and both houses of Congress are involved in debates about the quality of education and the need for student protection. Most of the proposals are intended to increase regulation of the for-profit sector and to provide increased protection for students.

The three key areas government has focused on are funding, accessibility and disclosure. Each of these are addressed in this section.

Gainful Employment

Gainful employment is referred to in the Higher Education Act of 1965. You can read more about it at: http://www2.ed.gov/policy/highered/leg/hea08/index.html

This Act includes rules that determine whether a vocational or career program can receive federal student aid. One of these conditions is the requirement that the program provide "training to prepare students for gainful employment in a recognized occupation."

"Gainful employment" has not been clearly defined, but the DOE is trying to put some specifics behind the term. The process has been quite controversial, and included several versions of a new rule that specifically addresses gainful employment. Still, both the criteria used to determine whether a school meets these requirements and the concept of "gainfully employed" remain obstacles.

To establish eligibility to receive federal financial aid, the DOE requires that graduate loan repayment rates must be 35 percent or higher and that annual loan payments are at least 12 percent of average earnings and 30 percent of discretionary income. However, in the midst of an economic recession, many schools simply cannot show the specific data points that some legislators would like, such as a debt-to-income ratio including the amount of time it might take a student to pay back a loan. Why is this so?

First, these schools, sometimes referred to as "last chance" schools, are often serving those who have had difficulty staying in school and may take longer to finish. Second, whether someone becomes employed after graduation is highly vocation-dependent and economy-dependent. To simply put flat rules across the board seems like we are throwing the baby out with the bathwater. In truth, the methods that the DOE used to determine that we even need a Gainful Employment Rule in higher education are still in question.

The Gainful Employment Rule does not just apply to for-profit institutions; it applies to non-profit and traditional programs, too. However, some feel the rule is unfairly targeting for-profit education. What will happen to students who need financial aid and are enrolled in a program that could be affected is not known, as is how students in under-served populations, with poor past educational performance, will be offered opportunity.

On the other hand, the rule will give students more access to fundamental data, like graduation rates and post-graduation employment data. Legislators are actively involved in the progress, and 118 of them have requested additional investigations before establishing the rules.

Many argue that targeting institutions that accept students with poor academic records and therefore a higher risk of failure, the government actually hurts hinders the traditionally

Dani Babb

disadvantaged from earning a degree. As a
result, online educational institutions in the for-
profit sector then reach out to those who could
not get into state schools, which ultimately
benefits society as a whole.

This is such a controversial topic that after
a draft proposal of the rules was released, the
government received a record 90,000-plus
comments on it, forcing them to wait a bit to
review the legislation while they read through
comments and weighed the merits of both sides
of the issue. Some of us argue that those who
serve students with poor academic records and
those who drop-out will logically have less-than-
stellar scores because of the population we are
serving. These are students that historically have
not done well in school. The ongoing debate
continues over whether these schools are taking
advantage of students, or providing a service to
the under-served.

As a side note, I worked in a couple of the
schools noted in the Department of Justice

reports indicating that enrollment counselors and advisers were unfairly pushing students to go to school. I saw firsthand that the quality of the students' work was lower at those schools. However, I also had a lot of students who were trying to better themselves and who also had very low-paying jobs as well as families. These learners who were simply using the schools available to them to make a better life for their families endeared themselves to me. That isn't to say a few disreputable schools did not exaggerate opportunities, deemphasize costs or encourage those students who were at high risk for failure to enroll anyway.

As a result of the Higher Education Opportunity Act, schools that receive federal financial aid are now required to post net cost calculators on their websites to help you figure out what the costs for attending that school will be, including all fees, tuition and so on.

You can see an Example on the University of Minnesota website at https://npc.collegeboard.org/student/app/tcum n.

In June of 2011, new performance requirements were released that institutions must meet in order to receive federal student aid funding. If they cannot meet any of the criteria, they must disclose this to students and then allow them what we would call a "right of rescission" period in business – a three day waiting period for enrollment. Schools have three years to comply with the latest set of regulations, meaning that most will be impacted by 2015. However, regulations are not only intended for the for-profit industry; they affect all higher educational institutions. You can stay up-to-date on these issues by watching the Education and Workforce Committee Website at http://edworkforce.house.gov/.

In my view, the Gainful Employment Rule adversely and disproportionally affects online and for-profit education and therefore, those who need a second chance to go back to school.

The Government Accountability Office has noted that for-profit college enrollment has grown from about 365,000 students in 2009 to about 1.8 million students in 2011 and a lot of this growth has been serving students that do not have much opportunity to attend school elsewhere, such as those with poor financial history or poor student success history. For many of these learners, this is their only way to go back to school and better their lives. You can read this study at http://www.gao.gov/new.items/d10948t.pdf.

The for-profit school sector is quite diverse, from small privately owned schools to large, publicly traded corporations. Many of us argue that this is a political battle and not so much a sound government battle. More Democratic lawmakers want the legislation, while more Republican lawmakers do not.

The Sloan Consortium has some great information and data available on the role of online higher education, the marketplace and students available at

http://sloanconsortium.org/publications/survey
/survey05.asp.

In 2009, students at for-profit colleges
received more than $4 billion in Pell Grants and
more than $20 billion in federal student loans.
Almost 90 percent of the revenue from for-profit
institutions comes from federal grants and loans,
so losing these funds would devastate the
schools and possibly put them out of business. It
would possibly also mean a substantial decrease
in servicing to underserved populations.

Department of Justice

The Department of Justice (DOJ) released a
report in August 2010 after it investigated 15
for-profit colleges and found fraudulent
practices at four of them. All of these colleges
made deceptive or questionable statements to
the undercover applicants. Four applicants were
encouraged to falsify their financial aid forms to
qualify for federal aid, by tactics such as
removing savings. Others exaggerated

undercover applicants' potential salaries after graduation and did not provide clear documentation about the college's program duration, costs, or graduation rate despite federal regulations requiring this information. This is some of the basis for the rules discussed above. You can read more about the specific investigation at

http://www.gao.gov/products/GAO-10-948T and you can view the full PDF report there as well. The DOJ released a famous video with actual conversations and voice messages from the schools being investigated. You can review these   at:

http://www.youtube.com/watch?v=4XZp-2HDRG0&autoplay=1&rel=0&showinfo=0

If you want more information about specific colleges, you can contact the Department of Justice Public Affairs office at (202) 512-4800 or by email at youngc1@gao.gov

What you see in the videos is not typical of online or for-profit education. But it created controversy, a significant problem for higher education, and prompted many of the rules and legislation that we have covered thus far. Many rules and new policies, procedures and training videos were placed upon faculty when these videos were released, and admissions departments took even more heat.

For Profit or Non-Profit Education?

There are of course many not-for-profit online schools that offer quality education. Many times they are not online only, but rather, hybrid programs at state or private schools. They are funded by private owners or by alumni or states in the same way traditional schools are.

In this section I'll mostly address online schools in the for-profit sector, as they took the brunt of the media's wrath and governmental scrutiny from 2009 until – well – it's still occurring as this book is published.

Some of it is deserved; some of it, not so much. There are a number of legitimate and solid for-profit institutions out there available to those of you looking to go to school online. In some ways, just as being "for profit" and having shareholders to answer to has led to greater efficiencies and product quality in other industries; likewise, being "for profit" has improved quality and standards at some educational institutions. Those that quickly come to mind are my own alma mater (Capella University), Walden University and American Public University System or APUS – but that is certainly not an exhaustive list. As a long-time faculty member at each of these schools, I have a unique perspective into what is happening behind the scenes at these universities that will affect the quality of education you get.

PROS – FOR PROFIT SECTOR

Standardized Classrooms	For-profit schools are under intense scrutiny to provide quality education

despite the economic downturn. A benefit to this that students will see is that quality often results in standardized practices. What you see in one classroom is what you will see in another; announcements have the same look and feel and the course rooms will not have as much "instructor discretion." We follow prescribed protocols, use rubrics developed by subject matter experts and employ popular learning management systems such as Blackboard.

For example, I can usually teach a course in one program at a for-profit online institution and then be assigned a course in another program at the same school that— other than differences in the specific curriculum—is so similar in look and feel that it takes me only minutes to get acquainted. If it takes me minutes, chances are it will take you only minutes, too. This can be a huge advantage for those that prefer familiarity and want to know what to expect when they first jump into a course.

Driven by Scrutiny

As much as those of us who teach in for-profit education (I also teach in other sectors) do not like the scrutiny in our courses because we like some things to be left to academic freedom (something those in traditional academia regularly enjoy), there is significant benefit to students and that is the scrutiny means that automatic and intentional checks are made on courses.

For example, at Walden University, if an instructor doesn't meet very (very!) specific login requirements, not only is the automatic system notifying our deans but manual course checks also reveal this. What this means to you is that you will not have an instructor who is missing in action for very long.

This also means that sometimes faculty are in a hurry and won't post as substantively as you may expect. Still, the rigor is there, and you will most likely benefit from this. If you have a question posted to the course room, your instructor will likely find it quickly. As an instructor who counts on income from for-profit education, I may login, post and grade work in schools that use automatic "bots" before I begin my work on another course at a different school. As an instructor, I can assure you that the amount of time these schools now require is at an all-time high and a lot is being said in instructor forums about the requirements going way up while pay remains the same or is decreased.

Intense Requirements for Faculty

Gone are the days when an inexperienced instructor with a master's degree will be your professor in a for-profit master's or doctoral program. Today, you can virtually count on getting an experienced professor with a master's or more likely, a doctorate. It's commonly known in education that if you are just starting out and not quite sure what you are doing, there are some schools you just don't apply to. The aforementioned three are included in that list. Instructors often begin at what we'd refer to as a "starter school", one with heavy demands that pays less and has requirements to make sure instructors are in the classroom, usually daily, such as responding to every single student's post within 24-48 hours (regardless of the value that it adds). Often the experienced instructors leave these schools to go work at schools that allow more academic freedom and expect the best from faculty without being micro managed.

Accreditation

To survive and flourish in the online or traditional markets, schools need to be regionally accredited. If they are only nationally accredited, you may find they are quietly working behind the scenes in an attempt to gain regional accreditation to improve their reputation. With additional digging, you also may find many of these schools would not hire their own graduates, because their graduates need to have degrees from regionally accredited schools! Irony? That is an understatement. Publicly traded, for-profit schools will do nearly anything possible to ensure they maintain regional accreditation, or national, if that is all they have. This helps ensure your degree will hold merit for your lifetime. I will write more about national and regional accreditation later on in this book.

CONS – FOR PROFIT SECTOR

Costs   As I noted above, for-profit schools are under intense scrutiny to provide quality education and, of course, to turn a profit. This means they may cost a bit more than other schools in exchange for their standardized curriculum and 24x7 student support system. It also means they may have stricter policies regarding dropping courses and withdrawing.

Transferring Units

You may find some for-profit schools are less willing to transfer units than other schools. Why this occurs has yet to be conclusively determined, but anecdotally, students assure me that for-profit schools are less willing to transfer units than not-for-profit schools, publicly traded schools, or even privately owned for-profit schools.

Stigma

In some market sectors, as you will recall from the data revealed in Chapter 1, there is still a stigma associated with for-profit education that isn't likely to change for some people or institutions anytime soon.

Some just flat-out don't believe that an educational institution designed to better individuals and help them "prepare for life" should ever earn a profit or conversely, that one attempting to earn a profit can have the student's best interest in mind.

I happen to disagree with this, which is one of the reasons I had no issue attending Capella – and so far it's been a terrific choice for me. After eight years, I'd surely have some blowback by now. I often run into students in my doctoral courses there who learned about the school from listening to me speak at a seminar about the pros and cons of online education. I have had zero students tell me that they regretted the choice or thought that the recommendation wasn't sound – not one. This is also the case for other institutions I work at and regularly recommend, depending on individual need.

Tips from Surveys and Social Media

I posed the question, would you choose for-profit education or not-for-profit education and why? This is what respondents said:

"Depends on what you want. If you want to borrow as little as possible, I suggest a nonprofit. If you want more student support services (and a better chance at succeeding because of those services), go for a for-profit."

~~~~~

Holly Sherrer Sprinkle

"It depends what you want to do with the degree. If you're pursuing a graduate degree and you would like to teach, you might want a state school for more teaching opportunities. A degree from a for-profit school might

limit your opportunities a bit. There are lots of non-profit private schools that are also good as long as they are research institutions."

~~~~~

Dr. Charles Thies

"I would have to say that I would be indifferent because what's most important is the curriculum. If there is a good basis for education with professors that have great credentials, I would not have an issue with a school making a profit. I have to agree that support services are very important but with my online experience it was the knowledge, interaction, and material of the professor and backing of the institution that made my decision, not costs."

~~~~~

Michael Hartman

"With the extra scrutiny being placed on for-profit schools on accreditation and alike, over a period of time, the quality and relevance of the for-profit education will be better than the non-profits. After all, it's about getting a quality education."

~~~~~

Tom Tonkin

What's Real, What Isn't? An Online Professor's Perspective

There are some very good for-profit schools available to students, and in some ways I am finding that they offer even better quality than not-for-profit or state schools. For students, the intense scrutiny on the for-profit sector has in many ways created more streamlined processes, easy-to-follow degree plans and stronger online social media associations for students to feel connected to one another.

Looking merely at quality, I do not notice a difference in for-profit and not-for-profit education with the exception of academic freedom – which is mostly an issue for instructors and not for students. For-profit education has had the advantage of bringing in top talent to attract students. State schools or non-profit schools do not have the same driving force and therefore often don't have the same success measurements. For-profit schools have been so heavily scrutinized that they are measuring variables like whether their students advance post-graduation in their chosen career field, or whether students are feeling stressors that could put them at risk of dropping out of their degree programs. These are measurements state schools just do not have the same need for. The academic freedom issue will come into play more for professors than for students. If we have a concept we want to work into a course as a professor, we will find a way – whether it's through a discussion board or a topic of conversation, in any course room at any type of university. If you read the discussions, you will likely be engaged in whatever additional information the professor feels is vital.

These measurements and self-regulations, regardless of how imposing they are on institutional and academic freedom, may be improving for-profit educational quality overall. If I were going back to school again, I would choose a high quality for-profit educational institution or a nonprofit private college that has strict measurement criterion and very solid faculty.

Some Final Thoughts from Social Media

"Make sure your computer software (OS, browsers, etc.) is up-to-date. Know that online classes tend to take more time than campus-classes (at least initially) due to the reading requirements, etc. Make a plan for the term. Expect that you will most likely feel overwhelmed for a couple of weeks

while you figure out what the prof expects, how much time you'll be spending on assignments, how often your prof is available. Expect that you'll need to be very patient. It isn't the end of the world ... it's just an online class.

:)"

~~~~~

Michelle White

Thanks Michelle! –DB

"I feel some of the best advice I can give students in their first online course is not to fall behind on reading and assignments. Online learning, while convenient, is quite different than learning in a traditional college classroom. Online course work typically has strict deadlines and falling behind can equal doom for new students."

~~~~~

Lanie Driskell Wright

By the way, if you want to interface with the Teaching Group on Facebook where most of these answers were provided, please feel free to join us! Our group name is Make a Living Teaching Online

Chapter 3: What To Look For In a University or College

As you begin to explore your options in online higher education, one of the first things you will find is schools claiming to be "accredited." But when you look a little more closely, you'll see that there are various types of accreditation and a number of different accrediting bodies. It's important to understand the differences—and what they mean to you.

Accreditation

Accreditation is one of the most confusing elements of choosing whether to pursue online education—and which college to choose. Everywhere we turn, schools that are nationally accredited tout it as something phenomenal; you might also encounter regionally accredited schools that disparage or look down on national accreditation. You may encounter nationally accredited schools that think regional accreditation is "old school". You may find a faith-based institution that has yet an entirely unique set of accreditation credentials. Ultimately you will need to know what your future employers will find respectable and useful.

Accreditation is basically a peer-review process designed to ensure educational quality. Schools must meet the accrediting bodies' standard; if they don't, they will not receive accreditation. Occasionally, accredited schools will fail to meet one or more of the accrediting body's standards and will be placed on "probation" until they address the issues and are re-examined.

Most accrediting agencies are comprised of scholars who are accomplished in their respective fields and have been in education for some time. In the early 1950s, the government started with a limited role in accreditation as it reauthorized the GI Bill for Korean War Veterans. The United States Department of Education, under the Higher Education act of 1965, is required to publish a list of nationally recognized accrediting agencies in higher education.

Warnings and Probation

A school may be put on probation for not linking programs to its student population, not integrating learning outcomes, not tracking faculty performance, may not have solid financials, may not be providing student services, or a host of other reasons. If a school is given a warning by an accrediting body, it usually has a time period in which to rectify the issues cited in the warning before risking loss of accreditation. The commission meets again at the designated time to see if the issues noted were addressed. At that time, the agency can remove the warning, extend it, place the school on probation or remove its accreditation. Schools take this very seriously for financial and credibility reasons and they usually are able to correct any issues that come up. If you are attending a school that has been issued a warning or is on probation, you should follow the process very closely. Sometimes schools are placed on "show cause" status, which means that the school must show reasons why it should not have its accreditation revoked as of a certain date. However, the college will remain accredited during that time period until it loses its accreditation.

National Accreditation

National accreditation agencies usually say that they hold online educational institutions to the same standard as regional accrediting bodies do for schools in their region. I have been through the process of regional accreditation but not national accreditation. Schools that are nationally accredited often also seek regional accreditation, though the converse of that is not always true. If a school does not have any form of accreditation, it is likely they are a diploma mill and you should stay away at all costs. (Many scholars will also recommend that you stay away from nationally accredited institutions as well, but we will get into that later in this chapter as online education has changed this a bit.) Regional accreditation is based on geographical considerations; national accreditation is not. National accreditation evaluates a school by its "type." Distance Education schools, for instance, would turn to the Distance Education and Training Council (DETC) for national accreditation.

Colleges of Technology and Career Schools may look for Accrediting Commission of Career Schools and Colleges of Technology accreditation (ACCSCT). A school may look to national accreditation when its academic model is different from on ground, brick-and-mortar programs. This type of accreditation allows a trade school, religious school or online school to be compared against schools with similar education models. The standards applied by the accrediting body are designed specifically for the particular type of school. The DETC indicates on their website that they are the only agency that works just with online education and hold schools to just as strict of a standard as the regional accreditation process does. Find out what your future employer may want. Schools that are nationally accredited can apply to participate in Federal Title IV student loans and grants, The Montgomery G.I. Bill and other programs for financial aid.

Some regionally accredited universities and colleges have policies which do not allow them to accept credits transferred from a nationally accredited school. This is very important, because transferability of units, which is discussed later in this chapter, is very relevant to most working adults. You would not want to earn a bachelor's degree, for example, only to find out none of your work is transferrable into a master's program because of the school's accreditation. Many regionally accredited schools consider national accreditation to be of a lower standard, although how this plays out long term with more schools online remains to be seen.

Some students have sued nationally accredited schools that have led students to believe their units would transfer to other schools when that is not always the case, or that their degree was of more value than it was. As of the date of this book the outcomes of these particular cases remain unknown. Some students argue that university representatives said their units would transfer and the institutions knew that was not the case. Everest College, University of Phoenix, Daymar Institutes, The Art Institutes and many others have been sued. This is usually college, and even campus or school (within the college), specific and not necessarily representative of accreditation. In some cases, state attorney generals have threatened to sue various online universities for not showing accurate completion rates or placement statistics post-graduation.

Is national accreditation really substandard to regional? In my experience, yes – but whether this is because of actual sub-standard programs or just perception is not clear. Would I choose a school that is only nationally accredited? Probably not. I have taught in nationally accredited universities that offered as high quality education as their regionally accredited counterparts. My concern is mostly for the transferability of units and the perception that still exists. Until that perception changes, it will be a difficult hurdle for someone who wants to, say, be a college professor. While both national and regional accreditation are recognized by the Department of Education, many schools that have national accreditation and not regional accreditation and claim that national accreditation is "just as good as regional" will not hire graduates with a degree that is not regionally accredited, posing not only a ironic situation but perhaps shedding some light on what those same folks in higher ed really think of only national accreditation. When I have asked Presidents and Provosts why they require regional accreditation in faculty yet have only national themselves and say it is just as good, they either have no answer at all, or say they are going to work towards regional and therefore want to meet those requirements. Therefore, I am concerned for people who want to be online professors who earn their degree from a nationally accredited institution that does not also have regional accreditation.

However, these schools do have their place and fulfill important needs. They often cost less and have self-financed programs. If your goal is to earn a degree to advance in your job and your employer isn't concerned with the accreditation of your school, this may be a good way to go. (It is also possible for a nationally accredited school to later seek, and achieve, regional accreditation which is very helpful for their students and graduates.)

Another thing to look out for: Some nationally accredited schools would not hire their own graduates as professors because they, too, want graduates from regionally accredited institutions. If you want to be a teacher or professor, national accreditation may limit your opportunities. Many students ask me, "would you go to a school that is nationally and not regionally accredited?" My answer, after careful consideration and hearing from those who think differently for years, is "no". Unequivocally no. Are many successful who do? Absolutely yes.

Regional Accreditation

Regionally accredited schools generally focus on academic degrees, as opposed to more vocationally-oriented programs. Online schools can, and often are, also regionally accredited; a big plus for that institution. There are six regional accreditors in the U.S. Each of the agencies covers a different area of the country. For example, the New England Association of Schools and Colleges works with schools in New England (Maine, Massachusetts, Connecticut, New Hampshire, Rhode Island and Vermont) for example.

The six regional accrediting agencies are:

1. **Middle State Association of Colleges and Schools** (Commission on Higher Education)

2. **New England Association of Schools and Colleges** (Commission on Technical and Career Institutions and Commission on Institutions of Higher Education)

3. **North Central Association of Colleges and Schools** (The Higher Learning Commission)

4. **Northwest Association of Schools and Colleges**

5. **Southern Association of Colleges and Schools** (Commission on Colleges)

6. **Western Association of Schools and Colleges** (Accrediting Commission for Community and Junior Colleges and Accrediting Commission for Senior Colleges and Universities)

As a prospective student, perhaps you might be concerned about those online schools that serve students worldwide and which region they would be accredited by. The answer is that the school's home state dictates which regional agency would accredit it. The six agencies above are the only agencies that can award regional accreditation. They are all recognized by the Council for Higher Education Accreditation (CHEA). CHEA is a national advocate for the self-regulation of academic rigor and quality through the process of accreditation. As of 2012, it is an association of 3000 degree granting universities and colleges and recognizes 60 national and accrediting agencies or organizations. Knowing that the agency that accredited your school is recognized by CHEA ensures you are not attending a diploma mill, or accreditation mill school, where scammers essentially make up legitimate sounding accrediting agencies to trick students into attending a diploma mill. CHEA has a database of institutions and programs that it recognizes in the US that you can access at: http://www.chea.org/search/default.asp or the list at the Department of Education, available at: http://www.ope.ed.gov/accreditation/

They also have a terrific overview on how to determine if your school is a "mill", which you can access at: http://www.chea.org/degreemills/default.htm

Historically, regional accreditation is considered the hallmark of institutional excellence. Increasingly, online schools are meeting these agencies' standards and are being awarded regional accreditation as well. Regional accreditation offers you the most flexibility in transferring units and the highest probability of obtaining a job after you graduate, especially if your potential employer is concerned about accreditation.

Other Types of Accreditation

You also might come across different types of accreditation when researching schools. Religious schools, for example, may have accreditation that is specific to their faith. The Association of Advanced Rabbinical and Talmudic Schools (AARTS), the Association of Theological Schools in the United States and Canada (ATS), the Association for Biblical Higher Education (ABHE), the Transnational Association of Christian Colleges and Schools (TRACS) are all examples. These schools seek accreditation from specialized or professional accreditors that are generally considered reputable by the U.S. Department of Education and CHEA. You can look these institutions up on the databases provided earlier to make sure you are selecting one that is accredited. It is important to note that if a faith-based school that has accreditation by one of these institutions applies for regional accreditation, it may be asked to remove religious aspects of its education.

Additional specialized or professional accrediting agencies you may run across are often industry- or specialization-based, such as the following:

- **American Dental Association Commission on Dental Accreditation**—for schools of dentistry

- **National Architectural Accrediting Board** – whose accreditation is a prerequisite to sitting for the architectural licensing exams in most states

- **Association of American Medical Colleges** –medical schools

- **The Association to Advance Collegiate Schools of Business** – business schools

- **American Veterinary Medical Association** –schools of veterinary medicine

- **Accreditation Board for Engineering and Technology** – applied science, computing, engineering and technology programs

- **American Bar Association** – whose accreditation is a prerequisite to sitting for the bar exam in most states, except in California

If you are in a profession, or wish to begin work in a profession that has an industry-specific accreditation, you should do some homework to find out what role that accrediting body plays in that industry and how important it is to employers in that business or industry.

Regional vs. National: Additional Areas for Consideration

Regional and national accreditation agencies do have some important elements in common. For the schools, they both take considerable time to achieve and require detailed reviews. Agencies evaluate faculty, school finances methods of educational delivery, the campus and the degree or certificate programs offered.

All accreditation is voluntary. It is certainly in a school's best interest (and most definitely their students' best interests) to obtain accreditation. However, a school can call itself an institute of higher learning without being accredited, though as I noted before, these schools are more likely to be diploma mills.

Some important information about accrediting agencies is that any legitimate agency must be not-for-profit organizations and cannot make money from their evaluations. Another common misconception is that they are government agencies. They are not. They can be recognized by the Department of Education (and should be a factor in your decision), but they do not work *for* the government. The federal financial aid programs allow both nationally and regionally accredited schools to use financial aid. However, if a school has neither national nor regional accreditation, federal financial aid cannot be applied. Be sure to check with a school's admissions department to make sure the college is eligible for Title IV (federal financial aid) funding if you need financial aid.

From my experience, most hiring managers don't know the difference between national and regional accreditation, though some savvy human resources personnel do. However, this has also become a hot topic among human resources staffs, so awareness is increasing about employees with degrees from diploma mills. If you attend school online, your boss may not know your school name at all. When in doubt about a particular school, ask a potential boss or someone working within the field.

Tips from Surveys and Social Media

I asked the following question using Twitter and Facebook social media forums social media to educators and students:

1. "Would you go to a school that 'only' has national accreditation?

2. Is regional required?

3. What are the pros and cons?"

You have read some facts and heard my viewpoint, here is what some others say:

"I would not go to a school with just a national accreditation because I want to teach and many schools require my degree to be from a regionally accredited school. If I were seeking a vocational education, then

a nationally accredited school would be fine for me."

~~~~~

Tena Hefferman

"I would recommend that students only attend schools that carry a regional accreditation, such the Southern Association of Colleges and Schools Commission on Colleges (SACSCOC), a regional accrediting agency recognized by the United States Department of Education. There are seven regional accrediting associations in the United States. These seven regional bodies, while purporting slight differences in accreditation standards, operate in a similar manner and are each recognized by the United States Department of Education (U.S.D.E.) to conduct accreditation activities.

Some schools carry both regional and national accreditation. National accrediting bodies generally accredit private and missions focused institutions; generally either career education or religious education. Students need to research what is the expected accreditation for the field of study that they are pursuing. For certain areas, regional accreditation is the starting point, but then additionally appropriate specialized/professional accreditation should be considered. Accreditation is important because it ensures quality, allows access to legitimate federal student financial aid and employer tuition assistance, and can be important for transfer of credits to another institution or application to further study."

~~~~~

Dr. Sue Kavli

"The majority of the general public is unaware of the different levels and types of accreditation. And, for the majority of people, I imagine accreditation doesn't factor into their choice of schools; accreditation is largely irrelevant. I have taught for nationally and regionally accredited schools in addition to institutions that are vocationally licensed by the state. If you ask most students, they would assume (incorrectly, though it makes some sense) that national accreditation is loftier than regional accreditation. The only situation I have had students be aware of accreditation is for adult students working at corporate jobs with tuition reimbursement (which requires classes to meet certain criteria). For teachers, and those working in academia, it matters more and can affect employment

options, so it is therefore more relevant."

~~~~~

Matthew A. Gilbert

"I would say that minimally you must go to nationally accredited in order to protect your investment in you. I believe that in some places regional accreditation may be an operating requirement, else it is little more than an additional expense that you as a consumer will ultimately pay for."

~~~~~

Frank Clay

"I was accepted to both regionally and nationally accredited schools for my MBA program. I was told that work experience and quality of undergraduate education carry more

weight than most criteria. If you don't plan to attend an Ivy League school or a top 50 MBA program, a degree from a nationally accredited school and substantially less debt plus work experience will gain more ROI. Going from undergrad to, say, Portland State for an MBA full-time will get you $50,000 plus in debt, minus work experience, minus a full-time salary you would have earned. I should note that I work for a large, multinational company and they have verified with me that an advanced degree from my current, nationally accredited school will allow me to be eligible for promotions/raises."

~~~~~

Jonathon Huckvale

Frank Clay commented similarly, validating the same notes about national accreditation.

"I think regional accreditation is important to potential employers but it may not be as critical to students who will seek employment outside the region. I suggest both are beneficial."

~~~~~

Dr. Arlene Blix

However, there are many other factors beyond accreditation to consider: Flexibility, residencies, on-site requirements, finances, transfer policies and your future goals all matter!

Flexibility

If you are deciding between on ground and online education, the key factor for you may be flexibility. Online higher education is often appealing to students who need to be able to take a course without being required to physically travel to a classroom. For me, being a business traveler meant I was not able to sit in a classroom to earn my degree; I needed to be able to do it from the air, on the road or in hotels. Online education was therefore my only choice (and is something I have never regretted).

Even within online education, you'll find varying degrees of flexibility within a program or between universities. For example, some schools will have weekly attendance requirements or even "synchronous" training or lectures which require you to be on your computer on a particular day and time. This limits some of the flexibility normally associated with online education. Some institutions, on the other hand, require little or no synchronous learning; students can move at their own pace and do not need to login at particular times. They may even be able to submit all of their coursework at once and move forward to the next class. Some colleges that focus on the military usually offer the most flexibility, and a few of these institutions also allow non-military students to attend.

Residencies or On-Site Requirements

Some universities have residential requirements. This is time you need to spend on-site in intensive seminars as part of your student work. For example, as a student I attended three residencies at Capella University, all of which were focused on research and included seminars in my area of expertise. They are often held in areas easy to access, such as Dallas or Chicago. Most online schools do not have residential requirements until the doctoral level, when a residency is more likely to be mandated. I have seen residencies as short as three days and as long as nine days. Be sure to ask the college's representative about any such requirements before you take the plunge, because it can take considerable time, be an obstacle to graduation, and be expensive, particularly if you need to travel a significant distance. And, of course, it limits your flexibility. Students with residencies though (and particular, doctoral intensive seminars for writing) come back with stronger papers and stronger work, from where I sit.

I enjoyed my residency process, although I did experience some stress integrating it with my work schedule. Residencies give you the opportunity to clear up confusing concepts, take advantage of some focused writing and research time, and network with your peers and professors.

Transfer Units

Whether a college or university chooses to transfer in units from another college is entirely at its discretion. A regionally accredited institution does not have to transfer units from another regionally accredited institution. The number of units the school will accept in transfer from your previous degree programs will play a significant role in the how long it will take you to earn a degree—and how much it will cost to finish. Schools will review your transcripts and then let you know how many and which units they are willing to accept. If you disagree, you can dispute the evaluation, but you won't often win the argument. Still, if you have your mind made up and know where you want to go, it's worth petitioning to have more credits accepted.

On the plus side, nationally accredited institutions will often accept units or credits from regionally or nationally accredited schools. However, regionally accredited schools do not always accept units from nationally accredited schools. The DETC has a guide for students on the transferability of units, which is a must-read if you intend on going to a school with national accreditation,. You can access it here: http://www.detc.org/downloads/publications/StudentsGuidetoTransferCredit.PDF

Note that this indicates that a school accredited by a CHEA recognized agency should not decide whether to accept transfer units solely on the basis of regional or national accreditation. However, many schools get around this by indicating the education from that school was not comparable. State schools are regionally accredited, so if you plan to attend a state school in the future you may wish to opt for a regionally accredited school only as they are notorious for not accepting units from a nationally accredited degree program, unless of course it is also regionally accredited.

Maximum Number of Units per Term

Some schools put a cap on how many courses or units you can take during a term. I have seen caps as low as 8 and as high as 20. Most schools will allow you to petition to take more courses at a time if you wish.

The thought process behind these rules is that students tend to be more successful if they're focused, and therefore, not taking an unmanageable workload. Of course, we are all different in terms of the amount of work we can handle. I petitioned to take more units in a term and was able to hold down four courses while working full time, thanks, in part, to my chronic insomnia. This is not a path I would recommend unless you have nothing else to do or cannot sleep! Some students struggle taking two at a time. You need to do an honest assessment of your own limitations. It is better to really learn and understand the material—that's the reason you are in school, right?—than to fly through, not fully grasping the material or learning from your professors and peers.

Consider, too, the level of education. At the bachelor's level it might be easier to take on 16 or 20 units at once, whereas at the doctoral level, this would typically require so much reading and writing that it would be extremely difficult to accomplish.

Length of Term

Each school has its own term lengths and start dates. Some schools have cohorts that begin every single week. A cohort, in the way I am using it here, is basically a group of students that begins the educational journey together, takes the same courses at the same time, and often completes the journey at the same time. On ground, evening MBA programs are usually an example of cohort-based programs.

Other colleges have monthly starts or quarterly starts. I have seen terms as short as "whenever the student can finish the work" to four months. If you lose your attention and focus on a topic after several weeks, you may wish to find a more expedited program with shorter terms. Here is another example illustrating how important it is to know yourself and your capabilities; this will play a big role in your overall outcome and satisfaction with the institution, wherever you decide to go.

I Want to Teach! What do I Need from my Online Program?

The world of higher education has specific standards that aspiring teachers or professors need to be aware of.

18 GRADUATE HOUR "RULE"

Rule is in quotation marks because some schools indicate this is not a standard practice, but it is "common." Whether 18 graduate hours are required to teach in an area of specialization remains somewhat unclear, but my anecdotal answer to this question as an educational consultant is "yes." The Southern Association of Colleges and Schools requires that graduate students who have primary responsibility for teaching a course have at least 18 graduate hours in that field. In my experience on curriculum and hiring committees for various institutions, 18 or more graduate hours are indeed required to teach in a specific discipline. If you want to become a professor or educator, I highly recommend that you structure your degree plan so that you meet this rule and don't have to go back to school later just to add more units.

Some students end up going back to more classes to get 18 graduate hours in the subject for which they want to teach.

Earlier in this chapter we explored the process of accreditation in depth. My reminder to those of you who wish to become educators here is that you focus on earning a degree from a regionally accredited school if you wish to teach. I know a lot of professors and university leaders who will disagree with my viewpoint here, and my opinion may change in the future as more schools go online and more students take online courses and more universities earn regional accreditation. Some argue that this bias is just like the bias against online education a decade ago and that in time it will no longer be an issue in education. This may well be true, but I have many professor-mentees unable to get teaching jobs because their degree is from a nationally accredited institution instead of the required regionally accredited degree. Ironically, I have noticed more nationally accredited schools unwilling to accept their own graduates as teachers because their degrees are not from regionally accredited schools; for this reason alone, I would urge you to enroll at a regionally accredited school if you want to teach.

FAITH-BASED – GO OR NO GO?

I am asked frequently if faith-based institutions are looked down upon in academia. The answer is "it depends." A number of factors, based on my "in the trenches outlook," are at play.

First, some state school administrators simply reject the notion of faith-based education, and question the viability of some of their curriculum. While this is usually not overtly stated, I have been in meetings where this was discussed so know that this happens in the real world. However, you may well not want to work for one of these institutions anyway! Second, some of the faith-based schools are not accredited by one of the six regional accrediting bodies, which may result in your application being refused if you want to teach when you graduate. However, if you are looking to move up in your field and stay at your existing company and purely earn a degree, this may not play a role at all. Ultimately, if you believe that a faith-based education will provide you with significant intangible benefits and/or a good education, then it is a good investment for you. I work at faith-based institutions that have serious academic rigor. Personally, I do not rank them higher or lower in terms of educational quality than others, so your decision becomes more of a personal one, not one based on quality concerns.

However, if you aspire to teach at an Ivy League or other prestigious private college or at a state school, you should take into consideration that a faith-based education may not be as respected as a non-faith-based education. Private schools may not be so rigid about this requirement. Also, in my experience, faith-based institutions tend to be most accepting of other faith-based instruction and degree-granting institutions.

Chapter 4: You've Made Your Choice—Now What?

You have your choice narrowed down to a few schools, or perhaps you have done all your homework and have picked one. If you have chosen an online school, this chapter is for you. I will tell you what online education is *really* like, revealing things that we professors talk about and experience "in the trenches"—information you won't find anywhere else.

What to Expect as You Pursue a Degree Online

The very first thing that most professors who teach online will tell their students is that earning a degree online is just as much work, if not more, than earning a degree in a traditional or brick-and-mortar institution. Most of the successful online students I have worked with share a number of critical traits:

‡ They are self-motivated

‡ They are self-disciplined

‡ They learn well by reading

‡ They communicate well in writing

‡ They take direction and written critique well

‡ They get the support of family and friends

In other words, going to school online is going to be a lot of hard work. You will need to integrate all of these characteristics into your own life as you work towards your degree. Your instructors will expect you to be self-reliant, determined and self-motivated. You will also graduate with a high proficiency in online communications, vital to your job search and career advancement.

I have been a full-time student in a state school, I have earned my MBA in a nighttime program, and I have been an online student, and I can tell you without hesitation that my online program was the most challenging and required the most work – and not just because it was doctoral level. There are many reasons for this. First, when I was given assignments and deadlines, there were no reminders from professors that work was coming due. It was solely up to me to factor my coursework into my busy schedule and to just deliver with no excuses. There was no professor for me to approach face-to-face when I had questions; I had to rely on email communication. You should expect the same in your program.

For me, it took an immense amount of self-determination and organizational skills to meet deadlines, integrate time to read and study into my schedule, and to do my homework around my personal and professional lives. You may find at times that your motivation wanes, and your advisers speak with you, but ultimately it is up to you to maintain your own motivation. You have to want your degree badly enough, something to keep in mind not only as you begin your degree, but also as you work through the difficult courses and motivational lapses.

At times, my program seemed overwhelming, especially toward the end when I was finishing classes, writing comprehensive examinations, beginning my dissertation, completing my research, preparing to defend my dissertation, and so on. It felt overwhelming. I found it helpful to keep a running list of every item I needed to do to graduate on a whiteboard, and instead of erasing items when I completed them, I would cross them off. Something about seeing the items crossed off reminded me that I was making progress toward reaching the end goal.

As you embark on your online education journey, be prepared to read. Online education requires a great deal of reading and the integration of the material into real-life examples. You need to be able to synthesize what you read and learn (and to learn the difference between synthesis and analysis), and you may be asked to work in teams. For some, working in groups is one of the most difficult and stressful aspects of online education because, like the rest of the program, the teams are virtual. Your teammates may be in different time zones or entirely different countries, and they may have different levels of motivation or time available to devote to the project. They will often have different norms, expectations and cultures. In my experience, team projects are more stressful for students than any other element of online education. They are often used to simulate the real world experience that students will get and to help learners understand the complexities and difficulties of working in virtual team environments. While they help students learn new collaborative tools, they can be trying to some who prefer to work solo.

You will likely have tests in your program, from quizzes to midterms to finals, just as you would in an on ground program. Some universities require proctored tests where you are watched either virtually or in person as you take your exam; others will allow you to take tests at home or permit open-book exams. This is often course-specific, though some universities have standardized testing rules. Tests are often timed and usually do not allow you to exit and come back later. In my experience, students who don't test well in person often don't test well online, either.

You will most likely have a textbook, and it might be an electronic textbook (e-book) accessible through your school site, it might be built into your course room, or it may be a traditional book that you order through an online bookstore. It may be a custom created book specifically for your institution or it may be a book that you can get on Amazon.com (and perhaps more cheaply too).

You will have some sort of lecture content, and it will depend on the university and sometimes even the course. It may be PowerPoint slides the instructor posts, videos from your professor or the subject matter expert who wrote the course, or it may instruct you to read specific elements of the book.

Today's online climate integrates more enhanced technological options, which are giving students greater opportunities to actively participate in the class, including live lectures, synchronous office hours, virtual chats and webinars. Certainly, technological innovation is extremely helpful to online students today.

You will have discussions to complete, and they may have very strict deadlines. For instance you may need to complete your first initial post (cited and referenced) by mid-week and your peer responses by the end of the week. Be sure you are very clear on when due dates are and what is expected. You may have a minimum word count each week, or a minimum number of scholarly sources you have to use. You may need to integrate a concept into your professional work or may be able to stick just with scholarly content. You may need to review current trade magazines or do research from foundational theorists from 40 years ago.

You may well have groups in your course, and you will want to reach out to group members often and early. Organizing your groups yourselves is crucial if the course instructor does not do this for you. Pick a leader and develop time tables.

You will most likely have an assignment (or three) due every week, with a big final project at the end. Your instructor may provide a rubric that will help you identify what weight each required component is for the total assignment points. You may have papers, case studies, presentations or some other form of assessment due.

You may have some live chat sessions that are required or optional, and you may have to work within very specific office hours with an instructor who is not on your time zone.

You will have an online gradebook with online feedback that will require you to not only analyze what your instructor is saying, but also interpret feedback so that you can integrate the instructor's comments into your next assignment. Every platform, discussed in the next section, has its own upsides and drawbacks. How the gradebook and feedback is managed is one of the elements that may change how the student perceives the grading process. Instructors will provide feedback and grades at varying times. You may have an instructor who submits grades the day after the unit is due, or one who waits a week or more. You will need to be flexible to work within that structure and still do your best work. Get a feel for how your instructor responds and when feedback is posted. Be sure to check often for notes so you can incorporate that information into your next submission.

You may need or be required to turn your work into Turnitin.com *or* another site first to check for plagiarism, which may require you to complete your assignment hours before it is actually due.

Platforms – What Sucks, What Doesn't, and Why

The platform, or learning management system (LMS), that your school chooses will have quite literally, a daily impact on your life as a college student in an online program. Every LMS has its pros and cons. It is important enough that you know their nuances, although what LMS the school uses is unlikely to be the deciding factor in selecting a particular college.

BLACKBOARD

Blackboard was the very first LMS that I learned to use back in the good ol' Loma

Linda days. I remember how clunky the entire experience was, but it has evolved tremendously. It is now the most currently used platform in online colleges. Blackboard supports mobile devices, which allows you to make posts and in some cases upload assignments using mobile apps. However, not every school has the mobile version. Currently, about half of the universities I work for use Blackboard. Blackboard released its first LMS in 1997 and went public in 2004. At the end of 2010 it was being used at nearly 10,000 institutions in more than 60 countries. In 2005 Blackboard acquired one of its competitors, WebCT, which at the time was its largest rival. With the merger it added 1400 additional customers. Current market share is believed to be somewhere between 60 and 75 percent, depending on which source we look at.

Blackboard went on to buy Angel Learning, and collaborated with TerribyClever Design (a company run by Stanford students) to provide the iPhone application for its mobile division. The collaboration tools it integrated into its platform are from Wimba and Elluminate, and its analytics are from iStrategy. Blackboard went on a buying spree to integrate the best-of-breed software into its LMS and many in online education believe that will not end anytime soon.

Blackboard also has other products that can be added on to its basic suite, resulting in a total package that can manage almost all aspects of student work. This is one of the reasons so many colleges prefer to use this product.

As of the publication date of this book, the most current version of Blackboard is 9.11. This edition combines some of the features from ANGEL and WebCT that educational institutions liked, such as collaboration tools. Blackboard, again, as of the date of this book, is still providing support to the ANGEL learning product and will release Suite 8.0 in 2012.

Technically the software is proprietary; however, developers can create customized course management systems using applications called Building Blocks. Blackboard hosts and provides software with a free edition hosted on their own site called Learn and Collaborate.

So what does all of this mean to you? It means that if your school is using Blackboard, you will probably have reasonably good support, the ability to enhance your program and flexibility using smart phone-based tools, you will benefit from the "ease of use" from the research and development we expect in a public company, and you will probably see frequent—and sometimes confusing—upgrades.

During the most recent migration to version 9.1, about half of the universities I work with that use Blackboard decided to migrate. Of those, about half again had significant technical issues that either required we grant very long extensions on assignment due dates to students, or suffer considerable downtime and student frustration as a result. The platform has issues in some browser versions, and when schools migrate from one platform to another sometimes the information and data just does not transfer seamlessly. However, discussion boards are easy to use, you can learn shortcuts such as how to "collect" a thread or mark an entire thread as "read" to save yourself time when you log in and want to see what is new. The new integrations with TurnItIn.com, an academic honesty tool that many colleges use, is fairly seamless.

If the university has decent hardware and bandwidth, Blackboard responds quickly, and it is easy to see and work within groups as well as find assignments and feedback. Most of the students that I talk with like the Blackboard platform and unless they are undergoing a current migration, most of the professors I work with like it, too.

Overall, I find that Blackboard does not add to the length of time it takes to do school work. If anything, its seamless integration into mobile applications makes learning more efficient and the money put into the application by the developers helps the platform stay technologically relevant.

ECOLLEGE

Some large institutions use eCollege, including Kaplan University and DeVry University. As the investment in a LMS is quite significant, migrating from one to another is lengthy and expensive, and often results in downtime. Some schools that have been on eCollege for some time remain on it today, even though Blackboard is considered by many educators to have a more robust, mobile-ready platform.

Some of the elements of eCollege that many of us who teach with the platform like will also help students. Quick access to discussion boards and a straightforward gradebook help streamline work. The system is relatively fast and responsive. However, it does not appear as clean or polished as Blackboard to me, and some students complain about that as well. What it lacks in visual appearance, though, it makes up for in speed. All hosting is provided by the company, making it an easy solution to implement for schools, although very costly. The benefit of company hosting is that slow Internet connections or old servers (commonly found at universities and colleges) won't affect the speed of your work.

Overall, if your school uses eCollege, I would consider it an advantage; once you learn the system, it is quite fast and efficient.

MOODLE

Moodle is an abbreviation for Modular Object-Oriented Dynamic Learning Environment and is an open-sourced, free learning platform. As of the end of 2011 it had an estimated 72,000 verified sites and was being used for about 5.8 million courses. Moodle is popular because it is fast, efficient, easy to develop in—and of course that it is free.

Moodle (moodle.org) was originally designed with the goal of interaction and collaboration and was first released in August 2002. The core of the Moodle platform was developed in Western Australia. The Moodle community is an open network of more than one million registered users who interact with one another, share code and free support. Modules can be designed by third parties and then downloaded by institutions.

If you want to know if your institution uses Moodle, check out the statistics page at moodle.org, which you can view anytime. The current version, as of the publication of this book, is 2.2, released in late 2011. Since universities don't pay licensing fees, they can add as many servers as they need to accommodate growth. . This is advantageous for start-up universities or schools that want to keep costs low for students, since eCollege and Blackboard are far more costly.

I have had good experiences with Moodle. From an instructor's standpoint, there are numerous settings we may have to change every time a course is replicated, which makes it a bit of an administrative headache. A couple of examples are release dates for examinations or weekly discussion boards. This usually does not affect students unless an instructor isn't familiar with Moodle and it causes a delay in getting the materials you need to do your work. Unfortunately, this is not uncommon.

Moodle is fairly intuitive and easy to use, and relatively fast if the school has adequate servers and bandwidth.

Students' forum responses can be graded while the instructor is reading the response, which means you could receive grades sooner in the unit. About 10 percent of the schools I work with have Moodle implemented.

SAKAI

Sakai is actually a community of academic and organizational institutions, as well as individuals who work together to develop the platform. Like Moodle, it is free. It is community sourced, and licensed under the Educational Community License. It is based on Java, which means it is relatively reliable, but in my opinion, it's also relatively slow. It would intrinsically not integrate well with Apple products either. Approximately 300 institutions use this software and more are piloting it. The following link follows you to see which schools are using it: http://sakaiproject.org/adopt. If you wish to sort by organization, click "Organization List" on the left side of the page.

I was recently involved in the instructor-side of a Sakai implementation, and it was one of the most difficult I've been associated with. Students who were used to the proprietary software we were using prior another platform found Sakai cumbersome to navigate; however, after a period of use, student complaints regarding usability disappeared. In fact, I have not had a student make a negative comment about the platform for nearly eight months, which, in my experience, is unusual for any system (other than Blackboard),. The system is stable and responds promptly when designed well technologically.

Where students initially complained about usability was the discussion boards, which can be difficult to learn at first. However, once you get through the learning curve (as you would likely have with any other platform), it becomes far more intuitive. My students have said positive things about its quiz and grading system.

ANGEL

Angel is currently owned by Blackboard. However, it is still supported separately and it is in use as an independent platform. The schools I work with that use it are state schools; I do not currently work with any for-profit institutions using Angel. Angel was acquired by Blackboard in May of 2009. The most current version of Angel is version 8.0.

Angel has a relatively intuitive interface from the students' perspective and, like

Blackboard, integrates student content into its site. Angel can be hosted by the university or the vendor, making it a low-cost solution for some institutions. Angel has Blackboard's commitment for no updates through October 2014, which means if you are beginning a program in 2012, it is likely you will not have to change platforms mid-program, easing potential stress for some students. Most schools I work with are on version 7, but version 8 supports all major browsers and is designed to provide a more streamlined navigation of discussion forums and gradebooks.

Overall, I have found Angel to be the most cumbersome to navigate and I have more students complain about this platform than any other, even though it does have some web 2.0 integration, meaning that it is easy to integrate into third party web tools.

The important takeaways here are to be sure that you know which system your school is using, find out if they have plans to migrate to another one (which could cause you grief later on down the road) and find out which version they are using. If you like your browser and don't want to change, make sure the browser is supported. Find out if your school supports mobile versions of the learning management system so you can access information more easily and on the road if you need to.

Tips from Surveys and Social Media

I asked the online student and online teaching forum members for their thoughts on the easiest and most efficient platforms to use for online education, and why. Here are some of their thoughts.

"I use Blackboard for a class I teach at the University of La Verne. (They

*won't let me use it for the class I
teach at UCLA Extension unless I do a
zillion hours of training - go figure.)
It isn't as intuitive as I'd like, but
once you get it figured out, it is very
helpful for sharing documents with
the students. It is good to be able to
post the PowerPoint for the lecture in
advance, as well as share
background reading."*

~~~~~

Pamela Barden

*"The most important thing to
remember about online classes is to
remember that even though you are
not in a traditional classroom
setting, you must still treat the
course as though you were. Most
importantly, block off time to do your
required reading, work on your
assignments and submit them before
the deadline. Communication is*

another key to success. Even in a traditional setting, things happen that are outside of your control; remember to keep your professor up to date. And last, but certainly not least, adhere yourself to a personal honor code; just because the professor isn't there watching you while you take your quizzes or submitting your papers, doesn't give you free reign to cheat or plagiarize other people's work. Not only is it dishonest, it is also easily detectable (especially plagiarism,) and can result in expulsion from school."

~~~~~

James Hargis

"I would have to say that I would be indifferent because what's most important is the curriculum. If there is a good basis for education with professors that have great

credentials, I would not have an issue with a school making a profit. I have to agree that support services are very important but with my online experience it was the knowledge, interaction, and material of the professor and backing of the institution that made my decision, not costs."

~~~~~

Michael Hartman

"*Walden was on eCollege and then just moved to Blackboard. I was used to eCollege. The Blackboard system appears to be more work on the drill down through the layers to get to what you need, and it's not as forgiving as eCollege (at least my limited experience)."*

~~~~~

Mark Vanatta

"My experience is with Blackboard,
Moodle, and eCollege. At this point, I
would give the nod to Blackboard
because if you set it up right,
assessment is much more
streamlined, especially when dealing
with discussion forum posts. I would
put eCollege in a close second
though."

NOTE: In this case, assessments
could mean discussions, assignment
and exams, so all things to keep in
mind.

~~~~~

Bill Adams

"Based on the ones I have used,
Moodle and eCollege seem to be more
user friendly than Blackboard. This is
based strictly on the number of e-
mails I get from students."

~~~~~

Michelle White

Your First Class Online

When you join your first class, you are likely to feel stressed, nervous, anxious, confused and maybe even a bit overwhelmed. Hopefully, your institution has given you an orientation, walking you through elements of the learning management system so you can find the syllabus and discussion boards. This is your chance to make a first impression with your professor and classmates, set the tone for your work and help link your coursework with your motivations for taking the class in the first place.

Usually instructors will ask you to share something about yourself, your work or professional life, your military experience and what you hope to get from the class. Be candid – if you are concerned about statistics, your post indicating so might encourage others to be similarly candid and help the professor understand your collective concerns to determine how best to ease these concerns.

In almost every course I have taught, the first week's requirements include reading the course overview materials, the course syllabus, the expectations for the course as set by the instructor or university (or both, at some schools), and may include a discussion board entry, as well as an initial assignment. Be sure you learn how to upload assignments the few days of class; you do not want to be trying to upload homework on a Sunday night an hour or two before it's due only to realize that you have no idea how to upload it. Be sure to learn early!

You will also want to read thoroughly what instructors require for discussion board assignments. Is there a minimum word count? Do responses need to be in APA format – (the format used by the American Psychological Association, which has become the de facto standard for scholarly work)? Do you need to cite and reference discussion boards or tie the work into your professional experience? All of these elements may affect your grades for these discussion posts which are often heavily weighted in an online environment, because the discussions take the place of the in-person communication. Be sure to pay attention to when the initial posts are due, as well as follow-up posts, since they are almost always on different days of the week, and missing them could result in grade drops.

Usually there is an "Ask the Professor" forum, but still be sure to take note of your instructor's phone number and email address.

Most schools do not allow us to accept work via email, so do not be surprised if your instructor counts it late if it isn't uploaded into the courseroom even if you sent it by email. This is due to regulatory and legal needs to have a record of the assignment within the LMS. Some instructors are strict with timelines (so always be alert for time zone differences!) while others aren't as intense about it.

The first course will also help you determine how many courses you may be able to handle at one time, as well as give you a feel for how effectively you write, how much individualized instruction you need, your overall strengths and weaknesses as a student and what your capabilities are within your available time and lifestyle.

Take your first course to get acquainted with the LMS, with the way the process in an online environment works, and to what strategies for completing assignments work best for you as an individual. This is where you begin to feel out what works best for you; working late at night? Working on school work on your lunch break? It will also help you determine how many courses you may be able to handle at one time as you get a sense of how well you write, how much instruction you need, how much time you will need to spend on grammar and APA format, and what your own capabilities are within your available time and lifestyle.

So what do others say about their first class, and what you should expect? I asked professors and students what they thought was the best advice for you for your first course, and what you could do to help alleviate anxiety and be most prepared. Here are some of their responses.

"I feel some of the best advice I can give students in their first online course is not to fall behind on reading and assignments. Online learning, while convenient, is quite different than learning in a traditional college classroom. Online course work typically has strict deadlines and falling behind can equal doom for new students."

~~~~~

Lanie Driscoll Wright

"Be prepared to be organized, and learn to prioritize your time."

~~~~~

Andrew Bomgardner

"Most everyone who takes online courses is typically a parent, a spouse, a worker, gets sick, and has friends and loved ones who are in the hospital and dying. Know that it is ok to take a break. Contact your Academic Advisor, your instructor. Keep up with the basics (discussion board postings), ensure that you have a passing grade, and request an Incomplete. An incomplete does not adversely affect your grade. Present what you can do and when... don't just ask for an extension. You know your schedule, your responsibilities; your Academic Advisor and Instructor do not. I often say, 'You

*can do anything for a short period of
time.' Do it! While I was in school, I
got up at 4:00 am, fed my infant son
(can you relate?), then went to work.
I stayed up every night until
midnight. Now, that I am done, I shut
down at 10:00pm because I know
when I work the best... in the
morning. I don't like getting up early,
but I know that I have more energy
and work faster in the morning. (I
have time to post on FB too).*

~~~~~

Andree Colette Brown Swanson

*"Persistence and patience are the
keys to online learning. Many adult
learners may not always be
completely computer savvy and bugs
in technology will occur. As someone
who has taught a few intro to
learning classes I see more*

*frustration in the technology than
any other area early on in the
journey."*

~~~~~

Michael Naifeh

*"Make sure your computer software
(OS, browsers, etc.) is up-to-date.
Know that online classes tend to take
more time than campus-classes (at
least initially) due to the reading
requirements, etc. Make a plan for
the term. Expect that you will most
likely feel overwhelmed for a couple
of weeks while you figure out what
the prof expects, how much time
you'll be spending on assignments,
how often your prof is available.
Expect that you'll need to be very
patient. It isn't the end of the world ...
it's just an online class. :)"
Thanks Michelle! –DB*

~~~~~

Michelle White

"I feel some of the best advice I can give students in their first online course is not to fall behind on reading and assignments. Online learning, while convenient, is quite different than learning in a traditional college classroom. Online course work typically has strict deadlines and falling behind can equal doom for new students."

~~~~~

Lanie Driskell Wright

Your First Class On Ground

You may be apprehensive about your first on ground course, which is completely understandable. If you are in a bachelors program, you may or may not be with a cohort of individuals – that is, where is the group of people stays the same throughout your program and you graduate with the same bunch. Bachelors programs usually have more flexibility on ground with when and how you take courses, so you may find this to be more like early undergrad education right out of high school, where student count is high and you are scheduled at odd hours (12 to 2 for a Bio class ring a bell anyone?!) However in a masters program you are far more likely to find yourself with a cohort of folks, like I describe in my own masters program. Often these are executive or evening MBA programs and classes that are offered on a set schedule for a specific period of time; between 18 months and 3 years. There is less self-pacing, and the timing is often regulated with one course at a time for a specific length of time. It certainly helps with networking though as you will become very close to your cohort over time!

So it's day 1 of class, and you are wondering what to expect. I'll focus first on associates or bachelors programs. As a returning student, you will likely find that the program is very similar to what it would have been right out of high school. You will work with a counselor to map out courses, take courses with other "kids" (often they will be), and work through your courses until your each a set number of credit hours to graduate. You will have assignments, quizzes, mandatory participation and possibly presentations. If you are in a "traditional" program similar to one right out of high school then you are likely to encounter different students in each course. If you are in an evening program for working adults, you're more likely to run into the same folks. Evening program students can expect shorter courses (6 to 10 weeks usually) instead of entire quarters or semesters, and you can expect a lot of work jam packed into one term. Most likely you will have one or more assignments due every week, and you will have lively discussions in which you are expected to participate and bring your experience to the table – quite literally. You will most likely have some sort of final paper or presentation, and will work on your presentation style and skills in the course. Focus will be on fundamentals; you will be going through the same 100 to 400 level courses that you would right out of high school, unless you transferred in some units. This often means more homework and more quizzes and less large papers.

If you are in an executive program or nighttime MBA or masters program, then you may find the emphasis shifting a bit - and you may also find the terms shorten to roughly 5 to 8 weeks. The emphasis may focus more on higher quality but less quantity of work, and a focus on how you will apply what you are learning to the practitioner setting. You are likely to be working on a capstone project throughout your entire program, a commencement of sorts of your work in your masters program. Sometimes this is a masters thesis, a large masters project, or will take some other form of large presentation. In many programs students are given 2 to 5 terms to complete this and usually with the same cohort. My own masters program required first hand research, and required that we show how each element of our program tied into our final project. We conducted a study and reported on the results which took roughly six months. It was similar to a mini dissertation. Each program will be different so be sure to ask. At a state school I work for in Washington, students are given three Capstone courses in which to complete a comprehensive business plan that ties all of their work from their courses together. You can expect that homework will take you much longer than in your bachelors program, even though the quantity or volume of assignments is often less. Usually each course will commence with some sort of larger project that you will want to plan for. You are likely to run into professors who are adjuncts and not full timers, and often work for big schools even if you are going to a smaller or lesser known school.

Doctoral students taking on ground courses often find themselves in small classes, with instructors who may or may not be happy that the student still has a career. In fact many doctoral programs require that students quit their jobs -- or as they often put it, "not have any other obligation side tracking them from their intense doctoral studies." Yes, often this means you have to leave your career behind. This is one of many reasons that while I had pursued my masters and bachelors on ground, I went for my doctorate online. Most of us cannot afford (in any way) the cost of leaving our jobs. You will find an intense focus on specific studies and most assignments leading up to how to research in a scholarly way a particular research question. You can expect to begin reading a lot of journal articles from day 1 in your course, and when I say a lot - I mean sometime 5 to 20 in one week. You will expect to be able to analyze them and find literature gaps, and keep an annotated bibliography throughout your program. The requirements are similar in an online program, but in an on ground program you will have your adviser or chair local to you; although, do not equate local with available!

Chapter 5: Staying Connected

One of the concerns that I frequently hear from online students is the ability to stay connected to faculty, peers and—after you graduate, alumni. I can assure you that it *is* possible; in fact, for those of us who are used to sharing about ourselves in an online environment, it may even be easier than in traditional institutions. It just may however require more perseverance on your part.

Developing Relationships

You will want to develop strong relationships with others in your program to feel connected, to serve as motivation, to find study buddies, and definitely for post-graduation networking. When you are communicating with professors, to connect with them on a professional level can be powerful. Some of my students have connected with me on a personal level online and have shared their goals, hopes, dreams and fears, as well as the trials and tribulations they experienced throughout the course.

You may find that the relationships you develop can change the way you feel about the school you attend and how you feel about the program after graduation. In fact, making connections is so important that many universities are devoting quite a bit of time and resources to create effective, cutting-edge, relationship-building platforms to help students stay connected and involved. Some schools rely on more traditional means,. For example, they will hold mixers in local areas, or have information-sharing sessions at residencies. Some schools extend an open invitation for students to come see the campus, although with students spread out all over the world, you may not run into many peers but you probably will meet some of your professors and deans.

Relationships to Survive the Program

Relationships may help you "survive" your program or feel connected, and not isolated, as you move through. One reason many students cite for dropping out is feeling isolated, which underscores one of the downsides to online education: feeling as though you are there by yourself, struggling on your own or perhaps with a small group for certain assignments. You aren't, but it is up to the online learner to reach out to peers and professors.

You may find that you connect with some peers on a personal level; perhaps you both get married during your program or have a child during the program, and build a relationship around that, or some other, common bond. In some cases, you may find that you relate to, or agree with, a particular learner's posts and find, through your online responses, that you form a scholarly bond. Or you may find that you have similar professional goals as some of your peers and bond on that basis.

Don't underestimate the influence of the professors and staff, too. Many students ask me if I *really* know my students. For the most part, I do. I say "for the most part" because some students work through their coursework, earn their grades and don't focus on networking or sharing, and that is, of course, fine.

The students I know best are those who take the time to help me get to know them; for example, by sending me their bios or responding often to discussions. Some students have come to me three years after graduation asking for letters of recommendation, and I can clearly recall their degree, which course I taught them, what their professional goals were and what personal issues they may have faced during the course. A professor I had at Capella University met me a couple of years after I graduated—I was his colleague by then—and he remembered me because during my course, my significant other was leaving to fight the war in Iraq and I had to submit an assignment late. (The first and only one I submitted late in my program.) He recalled how upset I was with myself that I submitted one assignment after its due date and what the underlying situation was.

So yes, we do remember. We do write letters of recommendation when we are authorized to (some schools only allow professors to write them if they are employees and not adjuncts or hold the title of "professor" instead of "instructor").

I have worked with students three or four years after graduation to help them get into the field of online education, too, or to find a new job in information technology (since it's an area of specialty for me). Some of my students have later become my colleagues, and in a few cases, my former students have become my bosses!

The world of online education is simultaneously vast yet very small; most of us who have been engaged in the discipline for some time know of one another if we haven't worked directly with each other. Becoming a part of that circle can have benefits to your work and your goals as well.

If you have an opportunity to meet faculty at a meeting, local event or residency, I encourage you to take the time to do so. Visit the local campus if you can, and exchange business cards. Keeping in contact with faculty and peers can help you stay motivated, too. I have had former students in other programs at other colleges email me asking for motivational tips, even though they had already graduated from my program. People who teach tend to enjoy that. We are your allies for life, not just for a course. Allies are good.

Tips from Social Media

I asked our social media network for advice for students on how to stay connected and keep their networks strong when they are in an online program.

Dena Rosko, MA-ComL, communication consultant at Text and Pixels, narrative researcher, photoblogger, and writer, shared:

"Make it a hybrid with one or two on ground seminars, digital storytelling, and group workshops. Then connect on channels including Facebook, LinkedIn, and Academia.edu, where you can search for academics via research interests, university, etc. Curate e-zines on your research topics. Post your work on a blog and share it in your channels via Ping.fm or other central micro-blogging hub. Research via web your research interests. Contact people whose interests or work resonate with yours. Do so in your channels and via email to schedule an interview via Skype or telephone. The latter builds

your network for during your program and post-grad employment while getting you up to speed on current issues in your genre(s). Produce and share content, ask questions, and talk to your family and friends about your work. Adjust your paradigm: Resist the cultural urge to compartmentalize yourself or reduce your journey to utility or job. Reject the 'real world' patronizing nonsense. Remember that real people exist on the other end of the virtual. Online education equips you to work on distributed teams and gives you digital literacy. Fear not the computer as you would not fear the phone (per se!). Instead go for relational, engaging, and vocational. This will help your health. Reflect on

*your gifts, desired contribution
(not outcomes), why you
need/want this credential, and
locate gaps in research that you
can influence for ethics or in
sectors. Then volunteer in your
community with your research
method/foci. This approach
builds your network and most
importantly helps you to
contribute your work in a
beneficial way while building
your portfolio. Talk to your
partner about your work. Let
them bring you down a peg or
two so you learn to translate
what you're learning. Schedule
meet-ups with friends, family,
and colleagues during holidays
and breaks to recharge and
laugh a little. Eat sushi. Drink
tea. Pray often. Sleep! You can't
build a network if you've no
energy or resources, so dig deep,*

*reach in to reach out, and keep
it real. People will appreciate
that. As for me I prefer sand
castles to ivory towers."*

~~~~~

You can also learn more about her hybrid experience and how it relates to education reform at *http://bit.ly/iinIll*

Networking for Employment Opportunities

The ability to network online takes some web savvy and time investment. Traditional methods work well as does email. Quite a few of my learners and colleagues check in to say "hi" every few months, and I welcome them.

Can we help you get jobs later? Definitely. A few of my peers at Capella helped me obtain contracts by vouching for my group work ethic. I have co-authored books with former professors. We know who is hiring, not only in online education, but since most of us are still professionals in our fields, we can often help you network with potential hiring managers. The market is certainly more difficult than it used to be though. While it is awkward to email someone asking for employment opportunities, it's not unusual—we expect it. Remind your professor or colleague where you met, which course(s) you were in together, and what your strengths are, and then explain what you are looking for. I suggest offering your mutual assistance and explaining what you might be able to offer, in terms of networking opportunities, in return. But even without this offer of reciprocation, you'll find most of your professors more than willing to provide whatever help they can.

Using Social Media

Today, social media plays a huge role in helping you stay connected. Almost all schools have a Facebook Fan Page that you can "like" and then receive updates in your news feed if you choose. This helps keep alums and current students connected. This can also serve as a fertile breeding ground for jobs. I also recommend following your school on Twitter, and following your peers and instructors, if they have accounts. Staying connected using social media will make your email asking for help a little less "out of the blue." Many have Google+ accounts and regular blog and post on YouTube.

Some students say they feel uncomfortable engaging with professors on Facebook because their profiles have lots of family information. One option is to set lists so that university colleagues, peers and faculty do not receive your posts by default. Another option is to have a separate Facebook account, but I would encourage you not to do that, from my own personal experience. Creating separate accounts has a very impersonal feel, it is high maintenance and with the new privacy settings, it seems to be more of a headache than it is worth (although that is merely my opinion). Still, if you don't want your colleagues or professors seeing what you indulge in on occasion or what you find amusing; you may feel safer having completely different accounts.

We once were essentially "anonymous" behind our computer screens, but social media has put a face and a life to the names we work with every day. I have taken a bit of criticism from school administrators who don't like what I post on Facebook or from friends who think I share too much with near-strangers. In this social-media-connected world where in online education, we work almost entirely online, this is our interaction and way of sharing our lives with others. Many of my former and current students are my Facebook friends, and we have been able to stay connected this way. Students know there is a real person behind the keyboard, and we know you have work, a family and many other obligations. There is a very real level of familiarity that comes with "knowing" someone in a social media world. I have met many students and colleagues that I only knew online in the real world and many times it was delightful, and other times – well – I would have just left it to online meetings.

Beyond alumni groups, you can also find distance education groups on Facebook (if you visit my website at *www.thebabbgroup.com* and go to "Online Students" and then Social Media from the main menu, you will find my list of hosted forums and groups) and in more traditional email-based Yahoo forums. Some online students have formed their own Facebook groups to share everything from candid thoughts about professors or courses to what they are struggling with. Some students fear that administrators or professors are "lurking" in the forums. I can tell you this does happen sometimes, but is less likely with a moderated, closed group. On the other hand, it is actually a very good way for administrators at universities to learn how their students feel about various aspects of the school. I know quite a few students use Facebook to help one another figure out how to post assignments, learn shortcuts to discussion boards, find technical solutions and so forth, when schools migrate from one platform to another. I have created groups for some of my students who want to stay connected to various programs.

Students and Professors have some great resources to share too.

"I couldn't live without Zotero for managing all of the journal articles I need for lit review and for assisting with inserting citations into Word. http://www.zotero.org/ It works as a Firefox plug-in or as a stand-alone version that works with other browsers."

~~~~~

Dave *(last name omitted)*

"Great APA/CMS/MLS resource- http://owl.english.purdue.edu/"

~~~~~

Charles Thies

"ratemyprofessor.com has instructors from both worlds, online and in-class, but mainly in-class. I usually check different forums, but everyone has to be very critical since some forums spread sometimes incorrect information. But I can guess what kind of school it is if the opinions are similar on different forums and former students express similar opinions. You can learn that way which schools just want to get you in and then they don't assist or they promise something that they don't offer."

~~~~~

Thomasz Mackowicz

While the world in online education can feel isolating at times, it is up to each student and graduate to reach out to others for support and networking. Social media has provided numerous platforms for us to do that and still maintain the benefits of being virtual, but on occasion it is nice to get out and meet people.

Finding conferences that will be valuable for your career and giving presentations to peer groups, and attending residency or even visiting your online school when you are in town can make your experience that much richer.

Chapter 6: Success as an Adult Student

As with anything else you engage in, those of us who have been in "your" industry for a while know the best practices that can significantly increase your chances for success. Your ability to be successful in an online school is largely based on your capacity to self-organize, self-motivate and learn from reading. This is also true in an on ground school, though not to quite the same degree.

You will notice a repeated word in this section: "self." That's because if you have chosen to go to school online, you won't have a professor standing in front of you every week telling you what to do and when, although you might have emails that are strikingly similar in tone! Most of you have very busy lives. You have to find time to structure your school work around your life, and that takes motivation and prioritization, and an ability to be—and stay—organized.

Organization Matters!

No matter what type program you choose, your ability to stay organized and on task may be the difference between a highly stressful experience and one in which you feel in control and ultimately achieve great success despite the stress. Staying organized means knowing when your assignments are due, scheduling time to complete them, scheduling time to respond to asynchronous discussions, attending synchronous sessions if your program requires it, reading (often, quite a bit), and staying networked with your classmates and professors. It also means setting aside time to attend residencies if you are attending a doctoral program or, in some cases, master's programs. It certainly means being accountable for being late. There is nothing worse to professors than students who ask for more time because they did not plan their week. On the other hand, when a student simply says: "Professor, I will be late, no excuse, I accept the penalty, my apologies" – that to many of us is respectable and understandable.

Most of my students have told me that they prefer printing out their syllabus and highlighting what is due. That worked well for me too, even though it is somewhat "old school"; one could argue that many trees lost their precious lives in my pursuit of higher education. I threw away each page as I completed the work in a completely and totally selfish act of tree abuse. This tangible act gave me a very real sense of progress as I saw the stack gradually become smaller and I felt myself more in control of my deliverables.

I also wrote out every single course, residency and large project (comprehensive exams and my dissertation) that was required in my program on my home and work whiteboards and crossed them out as I completed them. I have shared this tip many times with my own students who have found it motivational. A key here was crossing them out and not erasing them. By crossing them out, I was not only able to see what was waiting for me ahead, but what I had already accomplished when I was feeling down. I also taped a picture of a trailer on my monitor, reminding myself that I would likely live there if I didn't finish this degree soon. That helped, although required a lot of explaining.

Now I use Microsoft Outlook to manage the courses I teach, and enter requirements and a three- or four-day "heads up" before a major deadline into the calendar. I then have this synchronized to my phone through Gmail. I know many learners are using that method today, as well. Find what works for you. If it is a traditional day-planner from your local greeting card store or the calendar your local real estate left on your doorstep, go for it. If it's the most high-tech beta version of a smartphone app, use that. Just be sure you stick with it, check it often and set aside the appropriate time to complete your work. (When in doubt overestimate how long it will take you to complete a task; don't underestimate.) I have also found that a vital part of organization is letting others involved in your life (family, bosses, friends) know when you've got major assignments coming up, especially those requiring a substantial amount of your time, so you can get the support structure you need to complete them.

It is important to find ways to motivate yourself, too. Celebrate the milestones along the way, such as another quarter completed or a big examination finished. But if you are like me, you'll just keep your eye on that whiteboard, cross things off and keep your head low – which may in itself be your motivation!

What about tips from others, graduates, students, professors and deans, to help you be successful? Here are some of the responses I received in soliciting answers to that question!

Tips from Students and Graduates, Professors and Deans

"My greatest skills were time management, organizational skills, the ability to prioritize tasks and, above all else, self-discipline. That meant telling people that just because I was there, I was not necessarily available."

~~~~~

Dr. Paula Zobisch

"Set aside time every week to focus on your coursework. Keeping up with the reading and assignments is critical if you are both going to do well and, more importantly, learn all you can from the class. Also, try to relate the subject matter to what interests you. For example, I always try to relate the subject to nonprofits, which is my field of work. That makes the learning so much more relevant, and it can also help you on work-related projects. For example, one paper I did for a consumer behavior course has been extremely helpful as I

teach fundraising and advise my clients. Rather than randomly researching 10 websites, I chose 10 that provided list modeling for nonprofits, and the learning have proven extremely useful to me in my profession."

~~~~~

Pamela Barden

"The most important skill I used was time management. You must use your time wisely and establish routines weekly just like you would if you had a class to attend on campus."

~~~~~

Darrell Rice

"Have a backup plan. The Internet and/or power will go off during the composition of your most important *paper. Have other places mapped out that you can get to when you need an Internet connection. Have other computers/laptops included in your technology plan so that if you end up with a virus or drive crash, etc., you aren't completely stuck. Back up all of your work. You should keep your hard drive backed up regardless, but make sure you keep your important items in a few places so that if something crashes, you don't have to start over from scratch. Also, make sure you get to know and keep communication lines open with at least a couple of your classmates. They can be a valuable resource if you don't understand an assignment, or have trouble accessing something. Finally, make sure your computer always has up-to-date software. Most technical glitches are due to out-of-date operating systems and browsers. Have a few browsers available to you so you can avoid entering panic-mode--especially if you are not technically savvy."*

~~~~~

Michelle White

"Organize your time effectively and efficiently. Remember, the education will pay off but it may not feel like that in the moment."

~~~~~

Dr. Nicole Schermerhorn

"Time management! When it comes to online versus face-to-face, there is no a set time to go to class. However, I found that by setting a schedule of when I needed to 'go to class' online, I actually set up an accountability system for myself. I required myself to be online for

a set number of hours a day and week, at a specific time of the day that was right for me. If I had a schedule conflict on one day, I made sure to pencil in a new time to make up for the lost session. This was a successful tip for me that allowed me to complete my doctoral degree within four years."

~~~~~

Jessica Cahill Guire

"Communicate, communicate, communicate! When you're having any type of problem or issue, keep the lines of communication open. Most instructors and fellow students are there to help you succeed. It is not the competitive environment that most brick-and-mortar institutions are, in that for someone to succeed others must fail. The worst thing you can do is withdraw and try to work it

*out by yourself. This is a truism in school
and in life."*

~~~~~

Thomas Wymer

*"Read everything. When you first log in to
class, read the syllabus, every shared
document, every announcement, and
anything else your instructor may have
posted for you. If you want to succeed,
you must meet the instructor's
expectations. Each instructor does things
a little differently. Those differences are
found in the posted documents and
announcements. Keep an open line of
communication with your instructor and
your fellow students. If you keep
communication lines open from the
beginning of class, an instructor is more
likely to allow for an extension if you run
into problems later. Just make sure you
let the instructor know as soon as
possible when those problems arise. As*

for communication with fellow students, you would be amazed how much you can learn from them. Each online student brings their own unique perspective to any subject in class, and your fellow students come from very diverse backgrounds. Therefore, you will learn so much more if you keep communicating with them throughout the course, particularly through discussion forums."

~~~~~

Brent Ferns

"Don't wait until the last minute to do your assignments. Look over the assignments at least a week prior to the due date. Do your research then, when you are not in a crunch. Read and review the literature early. Then, if you have to write at the last minute, at least you have the research done."

~~~~~

Dr. Andree Swanson

"Dedicate certain times during the week that are absolutely, positively, no-exception study times. That will keep the work load confined to a block of time and prevent it from seeping in to every hour of your life. Also, if at all possible, find others that are also studying (the program they're in doesn't matter) that can help keep you motivated and committed. The camaraderie and mutual misery is invaluable."

~~~~~

Kevin Rawls

"Time management is essential for success. Like anything else, you only get out of it what you put into it. Therefore, if you put in the time to study, complete your assignments on time, and ask questions when you do not understand something, you should be successful."

~~~~~

Steve Rudolph

"Schedule the times that you will work on classwork and strive to stick to that schedule. Try to avoid leaving the bulk of the work until just before the due date. This allows extra time for "life to happen" and it will minimizes stress. Also, take advantage of the opportunities to interact with your professors and classmates. Discussion boards are especially valuable when there is a Q&A section because it allows everyone to participate and benefit from the information."

~~~~~

Rebecca Chipps

"A successful online student is internally motivated and a self-starter, who needs little supervision yet knows when to ask for help, has time management capabilities and the ability to set goals and priorities. He or she schedules online time, breaking large assignments down

into manageable small parts, avoids procrastination and manages stress with regular exercise and healthy eating. Traits that hinder success are procrastination and needing external structure and the inability to self-organize and stick to deadlines and priorities. I had a student serving in Iraq who was highly motivated and she found time to get her military work done as well as her academic work. To be successful, find organizational strategies that work for you. Review course material at the beginning of each course and set up timelines and 'to do' activities to stay on top of your work. The biggie in academia is personal responsibility. The program/curriculum is only as good as the investment of the student. Being responsible and accountable for one's actions is also prerequisite to being successful in employment and life."

~~~~~

Dr. Arlene Blix

"While adult students tend to be more dedicated than traditional ones, and most do well, not all of them succeed. The predictors of failure are apparent: the student doesn't want to be there (but must be there because of job pressure or they feel obligated for some other reason), the student is in the wrong program (wanting to make more money is great, but not everyone can be a lawyer, nurse, teacher, businessman, etc.), the student isn't prepared for the workload (family, jobs, social life all compete with school, and something has to give), or sometimes the student is deluded into thinking they can buy their grade (which stems from a few schools having such a deserved reputation of 'pay your tuition and you will get your A'). An adult student is not alone, and must make it a family decision to enroll; without the support of spouses and children, he or she will probably not have the time to go to school and do

assignments and studying outside of class. Faculty respect how a student prioritizes certain family events, and they appreciate how a job can cause a student to be late or miss a class occasionally, but school must be a high priority overall with few exceptions. Choose a school with a solid reputation (don't waste your money or your precious time away from family on a worthless degree that few respect); if you aren't sure, ask employers what they think of the degree from that school. Online isn't for everyone, so go with your comfort zone. Acclimate slowly; get used to the structure of school by taking one or two classes within your comfort zone in the first semester."

~~~~~

Dr. Jim Mirabella

"Getting access to the syllabus and course shell before the term starts (if possible) really helps students to become more

familiar with the layout of the semester and helps them to better plan their workloads, particularly when taking more than one class."

If this is something your school allows you may wish to contact your instructor or advisor ahead of time. Also, I'll add that many of my students share their opinions about how difficult a course or a subject was in online social media forums—another great reason to get – and stay – connected—DB

~~~~~

Dr. Kimberly Metcalf

"I think that student procrastination is the biggest reason that advanced degrees take longer than expected, or worse, don't get finished at all. When it comes to online education, procrastination can also be very expensive, since you often have to pay fees even when you aren't

working on your assignments and research papers. Don't set unrealistic and unreachable goals by telling yourself that you will finish a whole paper over the weekend (and then content yourself in doing nothing until the). Instead, force yourself to do at least one small task each day, at least five days out of each week. It doesn't have to be a big task, but get something done. A reasonable task could be to read five pages of a research article, write one page (or even a paragraph or two) of a research paper, or add three references to your bibliography. Even if you do only one small task each day, these incremental steps will quickly turn into a big accomplishment, and it's not nearly as painful as procrastinating and then cramming. Once you start seeing the payoff, it seems to get easier to keep going."

This is precisely what I did in my own program at Capella, too and it was very helpful! DB

~~~~~

Dr. Terri Bittner

"Everyone procrastinates to some extent. But the successful procrastinator plans ahead."

~~~~~

Andree Colette Brown-Swanson

"Some programs have minimum posting requirements for weekly discussions. I have found that if students only post the minimum, the discussion lags and is not meaningful. To maximize an online student's education and the education of his or her peers, the student must be engaged and active in the classroom discussions."

~~~~~

Jeff La Point

"It's been said before, and it's very true: there is no back row in online education. This means you have to be prepared for every class, every day, no matter what else you have going on around you, and that's a tall order. But a simple phrase doesn't sum up how to be successful as an online student. Here are a few quick points to help you on your way: Don't expect it to be easy and budget your time. Online education will be one of the biggest challenges of your life—as it should be. After all, the reward of your degree is worth all the work, discipline and sacrifice. You need to do whatever you have to do to make sure you get your work done on time, especially since you have to balance it with a busy life. Get to know the people around you, both faculty and students. Students do better when they form friendships among their classmates, and they do better in online classes (all classes, really) when they reach out and get to know the instructor.

Accountability, camaraderie and understanding are the main things you will gain from these relationships while you're in school. When you're done, though, you'll have the beginning of your professional network. And that is worth its weight in gold. Let your attitude shape your experience. I have heard more than a few college students saying things like 'I'm just here to get my box checked,' or 'I already know all this stuff; I just need the piece of paper to prove it.' Don't fall into that trap! Get the most out of your experience, and I promise you'll never regret it. You may know a lot of things now, but you're going to learn about why a lot of things work the way they work, and that will help you be a better problem solver and a more confident person. I can boil all of this down into six words. Be prepared. Be engaged. Be transformed."

~~~~~

Dr.Bill Luton

Throughout this section several recurring themes came up from people that I interviewed. Managing your own time and carefully selecting when and how you study is a necessity if you are going to successfully go to school and hold down other obligations. I have had plenty of students lose their relationships, significant or otherwise, in the process of going to school. I have also had students who were told to pick – school or work – and the outcomes varied. Planning school around other must-do's, like work and family obligations, is vital. Making certain you make time for your studies and making sure you take personal responsibility for your work and deadlines is vital. Going to school as an adult learner has an entirely different set of expectations than traditional right-out-of-high-school students. If you run into issues (and who doesn't) with scheduling and other commitments, share these with your professor or instructor and suggest a plan to move forward.

Personal Responsibility

As with any program in higher education, the keys to success are ultimately in your hands. If you are not getting what you need from the school, professor, group members and so on, it's your job to speak up and to do what you need to do to get the work done, all without whining. I say this not to be terse, but because chances are whatever you are going through in your program, those of us in higher education have heard or been through with our students a story far worse. At some point, students do have to decide to "suck it up" and really just plow through the work, plan time for unexpected things to happen and learn from mistakes or poor planning. Your poor planning does not mean you will earn a good grade without working for it.

From my experience, once you get into the mindset of "whether I make this happen or not is up to me," the ups and downs are far easier to handle. That was the case for me and many other students I work with. Remember, every class will eventually come to an end, I promise! I know that it is hard for a lot of us to imagine not focusing on grades, but I have not seen someone looked upon unfavorably for "only a 3.8" GPA, for those of you who are perfectionists.

Where the Professor's Job Ends and Yours Begins

Students have different expectations based on their experiences and the university that they attend. Some institutions are more "hands on," walking students through each element of a program or course, while other schools rely on students to be more self-directed.

Sometimes, the name that your professors are given is indicative of how they will be expected to work with you in the classroom, and other times it is merely a way to pay less. If a school calls a professor a "facilitator," that may indicate more self-direction whereas "professor" tends to indicate more of a lecture or one-to-many format. Mentor can mean a variety of different things based on the school or university. At the doctoral level, the term usually implies a close relationship working either independently on research or working in a high level course. At other institutions, a course mentor may just mean the person who guides you through the class. Although titles alone aren't all that indicate this, be sure to ask what degree of support you will receive, and try to match that with your own needs and expectations. Most likely, enrollment advisers will tell you something that is relatively bloviated, like "your professors will be available all the time for you." Some of us are obsessively online, but most are not – and I am sure when my daughter is a bit more demanding, I won't be either. You should expect to be treated as a professional, to be encouraged and get up front and relatively prompt responses, but not to have your hand held through material we expect and assign for you to read. Regardless of what advisers or admissions tells you, the fact is you will sometimes likely feel alone in the program.

This is one of the reasons it's so important to get in contact with and stay connected to your fellow students. I also suggest asking students in online forums, as well as professors in teaching forums, what their experiences have been at that school. Most will hide behind their screen name and be bluntly honest about what is expected from the university of the professors, and what they do with their students.

The amount of direction you get from your professors will likely vary with the level of degree program, (even within the same institution). For instance, a bachelor's student in his or her first year will usually have an instructor who is required to log in more often, respond more frequently and perhaps even hold synchronous virtual office hours, whereas doctoral students working on their dissertation will perhaps only be in contact with their mentor once every few weeks with progress updates. Usually by the second or third year of a bachelor's program you will notice the quality of peer participation improve, because those who struggled and were not making the cut have often left the school. In master's programs I find that by the end of the first year the quality of work rises; this is also common in doctoral programs. This is just anecdotal evidence. You can ask enrollment advisers what the drop rates are in each program – but you may wish to ask for flat numbers and do your own analysis.

Some schools will require their professors to "check out" work, and then use the "track changes" function to evaluate the work before uploading it again. This is becoming more uncommon as schools integrate academic honesty tools because these tools usually don't allow professors to work in this manner, such as Turnitin.com which checks for plagiarism.. However, you may still find that this method of grading occurs at some institutions, and even if not mandated, some professors prefer it. Other schools will have gradebook feedback components in their courserooms, where professors post comments and a score. Most schools today will tie each component of grading into a rubric for the assignment and more often than ever before, for discussions as well.

If you feel you are not receiving enough feedback to grow academically, or to meet course objectives, most professors expect you will ask for what you need. If you feel that more timely feedback would help you, you can certainly ask, but most institutions have feedback policies. If the instructors are inside those feedback windows, they often won't change their grading schedules.

It is important that as early as possible in your program, you really focus on writing, grammar, punctuation and, if required by your school, APA format. Most professors do not teach APA format, although they may point out some of the obvious requirements such as double spacing or margins. It is expected that you will read the APA manual, that you will read the course syllabus and the course materials, and ask questions when you are unclear about anything at all.

If you need help in writing or in research, you may wish to consider this as one of your college selection criteria: Does the school have a writing center you can make an appointment with? If you are weak in research, does the school offer librarian services to help you with peer-reviewed literature searches? These can be invaluable tools and departments as you progress in your work.

Having these skills at the doctoral level is essential. If I could tell every doctoral student one thing when they begin writing their dissertation it would be "the professor's job is not to edit your work." One of the issues that we commonly see is pointing out an error once in a paper, and having it remain throughout the rest of the paper. If your professor points it out once, be sure to scan the remainder of the paper for repeated mistakes.

We are here to help. We want to help. I would hope that teachers do not get into education if they did not want to help students with questions. Ask for what you need, and then take responsibility for your part. I have found that to be a winning success strategy.

Chapter 7: Technical and Writing Skills for Adult Education

Whether you have decided to attend school on ground or online, you will undoubtedly need to rely on a host of technical skills throughout your program.

Computer – Yes You Do Need One!

First and foremost, let's talk about the computer. I have an unreasonably large number of students who try to complete all of their homework from either a small handheld smartphone or tablet, or from a library. I urge you not to do this. If you are an adult student, most likely you need flexibility. This means you also need access to a computer at times when a library may be closed. You may also need to access sections of a course that are not available with a tablet or your phone. Some students do successfully complete their programs only using their computer at the office. This will mean you are not going to travel or take a vacation (which those of us teaching will not work around, so you still have assignments due!) during your program. If that is absolutely the case and you have available office equipment, have at it. I urge you not to.

At an on ground school, you will have access to computer labs where you can do and print out your work. However, you'll be at the mercy of the lab's hours, the availability of a computer terminal, and the available software. I highly recommend having your own computer, probably a laptop, that you can take with you to school and class.

Smartphone Access

The next question that comes up is one I touched on a bit in the paragraph above – smartphones. Many of the big learning management systems do have smartphone applications or apps that allow you to login to and access your course on your device. Blackboard, eCollege and Moodle are three that are relatively seamless. I find these very useful for creating a few discussion posts, but not so useful if you are creating or submitting an assignment. Chances are, you will need good ole' Microsoft Word, Excel, PowerPoint and other desktop applications and will need to submit an APA or MLA formatted assignment and quite possibly need a Flash player, not widely supported on smartphones. Are they helpful for quick posts and discussions? Sure. Beyond that, you will need an actual computer.

To Mac, or not to Mac?

I teach quite a few introductory courses for online and on ground students, and one of the common questions I get in the beginning of a new program is, "I have a Mac, is that going to be a problem?" The honest answer – sometimes.

Before all of you Mac lovers toss this book, let me explain.

Some of your professors will be using Windows-based computers – in fact most of them. In my own survey, 97% of online professors were using Windows-based computers (with a sample size of 210). You may think we are just outdated and not with it, but we need Windows-based computers because many of the applications we need to run simply run well in Windows or are not supported on the Mac. We may also have a Mac, but you may run into issues. For example, I have students taking my statistics course who do not have specific Excel plugins that they need for running statistical analyses. If they do download a tool that works (usually from Microsoft, no less) then they often have trouble saving it into a file format that others can read. This may simply be a user error during export, but can be a problem.

Also, sometimes I have found (and 82 out of 101 other professors found) that we often have difficulty seeing the same format that the student claims. Let me give you an example. This year I had a student send me her homework file with a .docx file extension. Great, MS Word should open this no problem, and did. However, I saw excessive spacing, errors throughout the file, improper file format and so on while she saw APA version 6. That was a problem. After several B grades, she sent me screenshots of what the same file looked like on her Mac, which looked as she had indicated – APA formatted. Regardless of which version of Office I used, I did not see what she saw. Most schools will let us adjust grades if that happens, but it's a nightmare for you and your professor. If you have a Mac, please do yourself a favor and at least get Microsoft's version of Office. Save yourself some stress, and your professors a lot of time.

Windows Versions

I have students ask me which version of Windows they should run and have (up to the date of this book) found by far Windows 7 to be the most stable and reliable, and most compatible with some of the tools and software installations you may need for your assignments. It is not uncommon for a course to have specific software, like SPSS for example for statistics, that needs to be installed. The last thing you want in an already stressful course is to have compatibility and tech support issues. I encourage you to use the most stable latest release of Windows (which means following our old tech rule and not installing a new operating system released by Microsoft until at least 2 service packs have been released – sad, but true) and then keep it functioning well with routine maintenance. And please, please always back up your hard drive.

Backups

Which brings us to the next logical technical requirement – backups. Some professors maintain that a "well timed hard drive crash" right when a final paper is due is probably just untrue. However, I can tell you it does happen "for real" as well, and when it does (not if) you want your work available to you from every course you have had. I have had hundreds of students over the last decade email me and ask me to go back into a course from a year ago and download their work and email it to them because they lost a hard drive. Not only is it unlikely I have time to do that, it's more likely that I don't have access that far back, and my student is out of luck. If you cannot afford Norton Ghost or another mirroring tool (in my view, don't waste your time and money on Carbonite, I will be lucky if my computer is done backing up from its first backup by the time my subscription has expired) then try a system like Dropbox, which also makes your files accessible by any device with the application on it or on the web, which is useful in its own right. Coming from an Information Technology world, I would encourage you to maintain USB drive backups, but not *only* USB drive backups. If your computer is stolen and your drive is next to it, chances are your drive will be stolen too. If your home burns down and you lose your computer, you will lose your drive, too. The only logical thing to do is offsite storage with a very strong password, and tied to an email address others don't know you have.

Software Skills

I teach a lot of introductory courses that assess a student's computer knowledge. If you have been in the business world for some time and use the typical Office products (Word, Excel, PowerPoint) then you will probably not run into many issues. The common computer skills that I see most needed are: Office products, operating system navigation, thorough use of email tools, strong understanding of Boolean search strategies, thorough use of an online library database (you will learn this in class if you do not know it already), and a very thorough use of web browsers and the internet. You will need to be able to do things like update plugins, listen to audio files, record PowerPoint presentations, and upload files to YouTube in most really good programs today. Anything beyond that, you should – in theory – be able to learn in your courseroom. You may find yourself using tools in Excel or Word you did not know existed, and be sure you have a solid understanding of the tracked changes feature in Microsoft Word because many of your professors will use it.

Presentation Skills

It is unlikely you will graduate from any program at any level, online or traditional education, without presenting at least one of your papers, research studies or case studies to classmates. When you do this online, you may be asked to record audio, record a webinar, or just simply upload a PowerPoint file. In rare instances you may be asked to present on a live call with other classmates. In a traditional program, you are far more likely to be asked to present your paper at the end of the class, a case study or research you have conducted.

It is important – regardless of the program – that you work on your presentation skills.

215

Learning how to pace your presentation (not only to hit the required and maximum time limits but also for the best transfer of information to your audience) is important, and knowing how your presentation is perceived and received by others is too. I usually recommend to my students that they practice in front of a friend, colleague or a family member. You do not want your 20 minute required presentation to end up being an hour, and you do not want it to be over in 5 minutes. Timing is very important when presenting. You also want to have the PowerPoint or other presentation format skillset that you need to successfully provide handouts and slides, and you want to be sure you have the necessary technology, whether it's a projector in class or a web tool online to complete the work.

Writing Skills

Writing skills are so important for any program, online or traditional, that there is no possible way that I could overstate the need to improve them – constantly. I am sure many of you have noticed errors in this book, and that is despite three degrees and two fantastic editors. None of us is perfect as a writer, and some of your professors will be better at assessing and critiquing your writing than others.

The thing to remember about online programs is that your "face time" and class discussion is usually written, so your writing matters even more. I see education—especially online education—as an opportunity to enhance your writing skills. In the next chapter I'll talk a bit more about writing and what you can do to improve your skills.

Not All Professors Are the Same

First, know that just because one professor doesn't find errors in your writing doesn't mean that none exist. It also doesn't mean that the next one won't, or that you should complain when your next professor's skill set is different than your prior professors skill set. What I am trying to explain here is that you may have Dr. Smith for class 1, and Dr. Campbell for class 2, and Dr. Campbell may find things incorrect with your writing, grammar or APA format than Dr. Smith. Please do not get angry with either of them – we all have our different skill sets. I am not an APA expert, but I know some of the intermediate to advance level writing styles to look for. However, another professor you have may find things I didn't, and it wasn't because I didn't try. It is merely because we all cannot be good at everything.

Writing Style

I have had lots of students come into class letting me know they are professional writers or that they have lots of experience writing, and do not understand why their writing score was "so low". First, most of us are not nearly as good as we think we are. Second, you are most likely used to writing for a different audience. Each assignment you complete may or may not have a different audience (noted in the assignment instructions, such as "write a memo to your boss" which then gives you permission to use a business-like tone) but your default position should always be an academic audience. This means writing in third person, or first person if your school allows for it under the latest APA version 6 guidelines. It also means writing with a scholarly tone and not a casual or business tone, particularly for papers. Some discussion entries will allow for the writer to respond with a more casual or business style.

Citing and Referencing

I cannot understate the importance of citing and referencing, and in the format guidelines (likely APA) that your school has chosen. Here is the number one reason: not doing so could get you in trouble for plagiarism. Here is the number two reason for doing so: it is vital to give credit where credit is due and is simply not right to not do that.

Starting with the first reason, if you quote a source (that is, use quotation marks around words) that are directly from another source, and do not include the citation after the quote (Author, year, p. – in most cases) then you are still plagiarizing. Let me make something exceedingly clear – even if you do not mean to plagiarize but you do, you are still plagiarizing, which is essentially academic theft. Many schools actually call it academic theft or intellectual theft or intellectual dishonesty. Many schools will accept an ignorance plea – the first time. But schools and professors are cracking down on it, and likely you will fail the assignment and possibly the course. Next, if you quote and cite but do not reference, some will argue it is still plagiarism. Not giving credit completely where a source, interview or reference was taken from is still academic dishonesty.

So how do you avoid the trouble? First, if you have a direct quote, be sure you quote, cite and reference. Next, if you are paraphrasing, you still need to cite where the original material is from. If you have a direct quote and you write it into your own words, you still must cite and reference the material. If you do this and never copy and paste from a source, you will likely avoid plagiarism issues throughout your program.

APA

Some schools use MLA format or their own formatting style, but this is relatively uncommon today. Almost all schools will use APA format version 5 or version 6, and most are using version 6. The styles for the most part are similar so if you went to school when APA 5 was in use you should not have too much trouble with version 6. Version 6 does allow for first person writing however, but not all schools have adopted that element. Each university and school has the right to adopt modifications to a standard APA style and they often do, so be sure to check with the writing center at your school.

The most important thing I can add about your writing is to remain open to input and try your best not to get frustrated. If you need extra help please reach out to the writing center. Most of my students can "see" the issues I note with their writing when I ask them to read their work out loud, so I encourage you all to do that. If you can read out loud to an audience (such as a family member or friend) who can flag sentences or paragraphs that do not make sense or flow well, all the better.

"General computer literacy is a necessity for the modern student. She must have the ability to use applications, such as Word, Excel or Powerpoint for homework assignments. It is important that a student understands the difference between an academic source and a popular source. Students must be able to utilize proper formatting structure, such as MLA or APA. There are many software programs that can help with deciphering the rules. Although this is not a technical skill the ability to read

*and interpret a rubric would be
extremely helpful, particularly with
time management."*

~~~~~

Rhonda Allen

*The ability to tailor a conversation or
presentation to any audience, whether
it be someone from the business side,
upper management, or a fellow
technologist. Soft skills are heavily
underrated.*

~~~~~

Michael Varno

*Students need to be able to efficiently
and effectively research. They also need
to be able to write at a higher level.
Some students think that copying and
pasting is "writing" and emailing or
posting to in instructor in texting format
is not appropriate. Rather, they should*

Dani Babb

use complete sentences and proper
English.

~~~~~

Sharon Johnson

As a recent grad school grad, I
understand this all too well. You must
understand the following: web
browsers and the Internet. Microsoft
word and excel. PowerPoint would be
good as well. You'll need to have and
understand how to use a laptop. You'll
need to know how to backup your data.
It sounds basic but I know of people, in
school, who have never used a
computer before. The Internet is a
mystery. These days proficiency with
the internet should be a prerequisite
for entrance to a school.

~~~~~

Eric Ortega, MSM

"I think it is important for adult online students to have basic computer and Internet skills. I have had many students who say they are new to computers and do not know much about them. Yet, they are enrolled in an online degree program! I also would like them to know how to upload an attachment. Again, this is very basic, but I have many that do not know how to do this. Finally, I would like to see students write correctly rather than like they do when texting (u for you; i for I; c for see; and so forth). Oh yes, and use spell-check! :)

~~~~~

Dr. Kimberley Diane Hall.

I would be happy if they could successfully use MS Word... to be able to adjust paragraphing, to leave the margins alone when given a template, to understand what a .5" tab is.

~~~~~

Dr. Andree Swanson

Obviously the technical aspects are important but how about solid writing skills? In today's online environment, I may not get to see a student to sort through body language so being able to express yourself well through the power of words is crucial for me.

~~~~~

Scott Cheatham

Online: *They need to be comfortable being online, using different types of browsers, and updating their operating system, browsers, etc. They need to understand that process. I am constantly frustrated by students who insist the class is not working/accessible for them or there is*

226

a problem when, in fact, they just need to update their OWN computers. (You can always cite whatever you wish in whatever manner makes the most sense.) It's okay if they aren't comfortable in the class portal yet ... they can get used to it in the first week or so. If turning on a computer is the most they are capable of, then an online class is probably not for them. They will most likely end up frustrated. Even though I post this info in my classes along with different browser links, this is the most common e-mail I receive -- "The class is broken!" "The tests don't work!" "I can't get in!" All of these harken back to their software being out of date.

Onground: *For my business-related classes, students need to be comfortable with MS Word, e-mail, MS PowerPoint, browsers, and even with any ecampus aspects. (My students still* *have to submit assignments online even though the class is face-to-face. They also use online libraries.) Be comfortable doing the basics on a computer so that you can focus on the class content without having to struggle with other class aspects*

~~~~~

Michelle White

Chapter 8: From a Professor: Tips for Success
(Online or On Ground)

This entire section is devoted to tips from professors – tips to help you succeed whether you are going to school online or on ground. For this section, I have consulted with professors from my Yahoo Forum, where more than 6,900 online professors go to collaborate and share ideas and to speak directly to students. Some wished to remain anonymous and some wanted to share their viewpoints openly.

What Has Helped Students Be Successful (Or Held Them Back?)

Our goal as educators is to help students be successful. We want and need to have students succeed to meet our own goals and to do our jobs effectively. So what has helped students be successful? Or hindered their success?

The first thing that came to my mind when I outlined this chapter was having a self-defeating attitude. I usually see this in research or statistics courses, which is logical given the "fear factor" often associated with these courses. Going into a course believing you will fail is definitely correlated, from my experience, with a tendency to do just that.

This also ties back to what you define as success. I have quite a few students every term who define success as a 4.0 GPA upon graduation—anything less is failure. This simply may not be realistic. I had the same goal and was very upset with my 3.94 doctoral grade point average. But get this – I had a boss tell me, "If you had a 4.0, I'd wonder about the quality of your degree. No one is that good." He had a point. Very few people are that good. Try to think of the things that really matter in your education--why are you in the program? And what role will your GPA play post-graduation? Once you can define success for yourself, I encourage you to share it in your introductory bio if the course calls for one. This can also help your professor understand what you are looking to get out of the course.

One of the biggest concerns I have is when learners immediately become defensive when I offer suggestions or when they do not earn an A in my class. A learner who tells me "my last professor didn't tell me this was an issue so you can't tell me it is now," is really communicating to me that he or she may very well have had a professor who not only failed to point out the problem in that course, but also that he or she is resistant to feedback. We are not good at everything. You may have one professor very strong in one area and weak in another, and will therefore get more feedback on the area he or she is strong in. This is normal and will help you grow academically if you are open to it. Without incorporating feedback (and sometimes we don't always agree with our professors; I had plenty I disagreed with, too) into your future work, you are doing yourself a disservice in the learning process and lessening the chance at that coveted high GPA. I have had learners tell me all sorts of things, from "I do not want to use APA because I do not like psychology so you cannot grade me on it" to "I didn't have time to re-read my work so you cannot hold that against me." (Remember the personal responsibility component of education – online or on ground!)

I have had students completely turn around mid-term and come back from a failing grade to earn a reasonably good grade, and students who have had personal issues come up that caused them to go from a good grade to a near-failing grade. Try to be kind to yourself. Remember, you choose to go back to school and school has to fit around your life, which implies you have an outside life. Therefore, it is likely that the aforementioned life will get in "the way" of what you'd like to do in school sometimes.

True wisdom is shared here from **Dr. Bill Luton** with advice for those of you wondering what professors are thinking and looking for and how to earn the best possible grade, whether you are online or on ground student:

It's pretty simple… when you submit work for me to grade, make it hard for me to miss the fact that you got the job done. How do you do that? There's an old saying about public speaking that says to tell them what you're going to say, say it, and then tell them what you said. The same thing goes for written work. Start with a strong introduction that tells me clearly and specifically that you are about to address everything the assignment requires. End with a strong conclusion that reminds me that you addressed those things.

But the magic is in the middle. For example, if you have four specific things to address in a paper, set your entire paper up based on those four requirements. If you're asked to analyze the two top-selling cars in America as one of your four requirements, your first heading should be "Analysis of the Top Two Cars in America." Then, one by one, give me what I've asked for, and you'll make it almost impossible for me to miss. If you decide to use subheadings for each of the two top cars... even better!

As a good professor, I should be able to find your analysis in there one way or another, but as a good student, you should want to make that as easy as possible. In the end, I should be able to put one finger on the rubric, the other on your paper, and match them up with ease. To sum it up in one sentence, think of it like this... give me exactly what I ask for, and make it so obvious that it's impossible for me to miss.

Organization

The most successful students I have worked are organized from the moment they enter class. They introduce themselves, they read the syllabus first day, they ask pertinent questions, they scan the course room for missing material, and they quickly jump into group discussions. If a student asks me "when is my discussion due?" and it's written in two places, my concern for the student's ability to succeed in the class rises. The more organized you can be from the beginning of class; the better off you will be throughout the entire class. As one student told me, "even if I don't meet the deadlines, at least I know when they are."

Dr. Kimberly Metcalf has some great organizational advice:

"Print a PDF chart of the assignments and due dates as well as the syllabus. When designing a

course, this is the very first thing that I create – a list of all of the readings and assignments for each week in the term. I then use this chart to put together the weekly instruction and the assignment links for the course, etc. By following the chart, I assure that the assignments and the due dates are all consistent from the chart to the course shell. This chart is also extremely helpful to me as the instructor because during the term I use it to look ahead and plan my work for the upcoming week."

If good professors are taking the time to create something like this, most likely it will help you tremendously---DB

Excuses

Ask any professor who has been in education for a while about excuses and you will get plenty of stories! In fact, it's consistently one of the most humorous aspects of the online professor Yahoo forum I mentioned before. Yes, professors do have their own groups within most university systems where we joke about these things; we need to vent, too. We have to, because we hear them every day, and if we didn't compare notes, we would likely lose our minds.

I have had a student who forgot she had me two terms earlier, who told me that her mother died—forgetting that she had told me the same thing in the previous course. I wanted to give her the benefit of the doubt, thinking that perhaps she had a stepmother, a close mother-in-law, a woman close to her who is like a mother and so on – but no – she described the death in detail exactly as she had done before. I had the old email, forwarded it to her, and told her that her statistics paper that term should be on the likelihood of this occurring twice in her life. She called me and apologized and told me she made it up—both times. Unfortunately this is not all that uncommon. I would estimate it happens in a very serious way probably 40 times in a year.

While this may seem irrelevant because so few people would ever do such a thing, it brings up a very important point. Your professors do remember. We take your concerns and your worries and the things going on in your life very seriously. If you are telling us something has happened, please be honest about it. You do not need to share all of the details if you do not want to of course; that is entirely up to you.

Among the most common excuses I hear are:

‡ *My hard drive died. (Please have backups. However, we do understand that "things happen.")*

‡ *My laptop was stolen.*

‡ *My house caught fire. (One student thought that her email about a house fire in one city accompanied by a newspaper article of a house in another state might convince me. I asked her about the article and she admitted she had made the entire thing up. I would not have questioned it at all if the article wasn't from a different state!).*

‡ *I ran out of time.*

‡ *The system crashed. (You do realize that you can always submit the work early if you like!)*

‡ *My Internet access failed. (Please go to a library or Starbucks!) This is most amusing when they are emailing me from the Internet.*

‡ *Word doesn't work. (I am still unclear as to what this means, but hear it pretty often.)*

‡ *I could not email you the file. (We don't accept submissions using email, anyway.)*

Dr. Terri Bittner adds an event to the mix:

"I had a student who had the same relative die twice during the same semester! Of course, each death necessitated a long extension on a homework assignment so that the student could attend the funeral and properly grieve. While it was rather humorous to see the student get caught in such a blatant lie, the second 'death' obviously didn't gain my sympathy, and the 'gods of partial credit' were not smiling at exam time."

Here are some other excuses that were posted in our social media forums, noted anonymously due to the nature of the content. We kid you not, we really did receive these!

 ‡ *"Sir I think my assignment may have been stuck in my spam folder so that's why you didn't get. I think."*

 ‡ *"I couldn't take the test because my father passed away."* *When asked for an obituary for proof, the student replied, "Oh, never mind then."*

 ‡ *"I don't like to re-invent the wheel. So here is a copy of someone else's work I found online."*

A student was a no-show until three weeks into a five-and-a-half-week course and said,

‡ *"I'm sorry I haven't replied the past two weeks. I was detained while trying to get back into the country, but I'm sure I will be able to catch up."*

A professor notes:

"I had one student who missed three weeks of class because he was in jail. He got arrested in a raid. His girlfriend was across the street when the raid took place and recorded it. She uploaded it on YouTube and gave me the link. Sure enough, that was him; they had handcuffed coming out of the house."

The morning after an assignment was due:

‡ *"I was kidnapped by my ex and taken out of state for the whole*

*weekend. I'm okay now. Can I
email you my assignment later
this week?"*

This was from a student that was emailing and sometimes even instant messaging in the class itself, in a course that did not allow for smart devices to login – so he or she had internet.

‡ *"I cannot submit my work because
I do not have the Internet."*

‡ *"My house was broken into last
night and they took everything,
including the notebook my
homework was in."*

Yes, this was an online class and I highly doubt they had a handwritten draft in a notebook. I guess it didn't dawn on them that "My computer was stolen" may have been a bit more realistic.

‡ *"I can't turn in the paper due tonight because I have to sing in the church choir this weekend."*

‡ *"I used the wrong book for the exam...can I take it over?"*

‡ *"I'm sorry, but I have dedicated too much time on this one project. I missed points in my other class because I was concentrating on your class."*

‡ *"I was stuck on an island and had to use my assignment paper as something to burn for the fire. My life depended on it!"*

One student commented that she had forgotten she was in the course, as if she were so busy with work and school, she forgot she was even taking the class.

‡   *"I was on vacation with my*
     family."'

One student plagiarized two discussion posts in one week. The posts were elegant, extensive and accurate when discussing two complex plays. The style did not fit previous posts. A plagiarism checker confirmed that the posts were 99 percent unoriginal, and the student failed. His response?

‡   *"It wasn't me! I sent my*
     assignment to my brother who
     lives in Colorado because he
     has a higher level of English
     than me. English is not in my
     veins or bones but it is in his.
     Sometimes he completely
     changes my work. I will tell
     him to be more careful to cite
     the work next time."

‡ *"The assignment was a waste*
of time so I didn't do it. Why are
you failing me?"

One student, over the course of 12 weeks, had multiple deaths in the family. By the end of the semester, he had lost four grandmothers.

‡ *"I have not been able to focus*
on my assignments for two
weeks. I had a very close death
in the family: my cat died."

‡ *"Well the other student must*
have hacked into my
gradebook and downloaded my
assignment. I don't know how
we submitted the same paper. I
did not give it to him."

‡ *"I was devastated when I lost a*
pet. I cried when my
grandmother died but a pet

dying is much worse than family!"

‡ *"I was too drunk to drive to class and I couldn't find anyone to take me."*

We do know that things happen that are legitimate. Brent Ferns noted that one of his students had to give birth in a car on the way to the hospital and she included a newspaper clip to show him. We have diverse students and diverse, real-life events happen. I learned that the hard way in 2010 when I was in the hospital and then suddenly in surgery. Most of the time, if your issue sounds plausible, we won't ask for information or documentation and in some cases, we aren't authorized or legally allowed to. We also aren't obligated to grant you more time on your assignments beyond what we agree to in our syllabus or university guidelines, if there are any.

Time Management

It is up to you to manage your own time, particularly if you are taking a course online. A professor is not in class with you daily or weekly to remind you what to do, offer you time to do your group work in class and so on. Your ability to manage your time throughout the week—and not submit a poorly edited paper at 11:59 pm for a midnight deadline—is vital. If you do submit your work at the last minute, and do not do a thorough job, you should expect, and accept, the corresponding grade hit. Part of what you are demonstrating by earning your degree online is that you can manage your own time, you are independent, and you have goals as well as the strategies to achieve them: all valuable traits that employers look for in employees.

Dr. David Gould, Core Faculty in the School of Management at Walden University, has great advice:

"One time-management tip I offer

*students is to use project
management tools, such as
Microsoft Project, to plan and track
progress in their course or in large-
scale projects like theses or
dissertations. Other time-
management tips I offer are to say
no to everything you can and
outsource the rest. No one will give
you time to work on your studies, so
you have to take it."*

This is perhaps the most candid and practical advice I have read about education.

Dr. Kimberly Metcalf adds some valuable advice for staying organized:

*"Ahead of the start date, review the
course requirements regarding
discussion board posting,
assignments, and very important,*

grading policies, etc. I recommend creating a binder or an online set of folders with one section provided for each week of the term. Then, place the weekly assignments and discussion board requirements in the appropriate weekly location. I think this familiarizes the students with the course and helps to keep them organized. It's extremely important to print off the term assignment chart and highlight things or cross them off as they are completed. The real benefit of having this information offline is that if students experiences Internet access problems, they can still work during the downtime. If they only rely on accessing things via the school course shell, they may not always be able to take advantage of an unplanned opportunity to get some work done."

Terrific advice, particularly as many of us in online education hear that work could not be done because the system was down or the Internet was out.

Once in a while, we get someone whose work ethic and ability to stay diligent in their course is mind boggling.

Andree Colette Brown Swanson shared the following:

"The story that I will always remember occurred over a 4th of July holiday. I was teaching a class and a paper was due. My student had travelled from Tennessee to Duke University in North Carolina where her son was undergoing a medical procedure. All the while, back in Tennessee, her family was celebrating Independence Day. In a fluke accident, her other son was

riding in the back of a pick-up truck
driving to her parents' house on a
dirt road—no drinking or horseplay
was involved. The truck hit a bump;
he was ejected from the bed of the
truck, hit his head on a rock, and
subsequently died. She shared this
story with me and submitted her
final essay. This heartbreaking
scenario reminded me that those
who choose to succeed do, no
matter what obstacle gets in their
way."

Read the Material Before Asking Questions

One of the things I hear most often is that a student could not find information he or she was looking for. Most of the time the information is in the syllabus or weekly reading material and simply needs to be read! We know you are busy and have limited time, but we write syllabi and produce material so you can leave the class with a particular skillset and certain objectives met. If you do not read the material we write (or that a subject matter expert writes) then you are not getting the most from your course. We are more than happy to help you find information or understand material more thoroughly, but please read the material first. It will save time and stress—for both student and professor.

Steve Strickland *said:*

> *"I did my entire BS and MS online (Dr. Babb was an instructor of mine too). I would say plan! Organize! Focus! It's very easy to be distracted doing online courses. TV, kids, Facebook etc....you must set aside time and find your zone. Once you do, focus. Use your computer to keep everything organized. Use your online resources (from the school and outside the class) to keep organized too."*

Writing Skills

In Chapter 7 I talked about how critical your writing skills are to your success in your online program. However, many learners are very stressed about their writing skills. I highly recommend writing centers or tutors wherever they are available. Ask your professors for feedback, but remember that some may say "please watch spelling and grammar" but usually won't correct your work unless it's an English professor in an English class. Writing centers will often make such detailed corrections however.

Invest in an APA manual and perhaps bibliography software if you need to, so that you can spend time on your content and not on formatting. This has saved many students a great deal of time.

Dr. Terri Bittner adds vital information on this point:

"The biggest struggle my students have is that many of them have never learned to write properly, and this includes students who have master's degrees in subjects that should have required them to do a lot of writing. I have had experiences where I've written extensive comments on a student's paper, only to have the student reply, 'Why do you have a problem with my writing? None of my other professors ever had a problem with my writing!' Students in this situation should realize that an instructor who takes the time to make comments actually cares, and is trying to help you. The reason that students may not have had many comments in the past is generally not that their papers were perfect. Rather, the issue is probably that the instructors didn't have the time (or inclination) to read through the papers thoroughly and take time to make many comments.

Don't criticize your professors for making comments. Appreciate the help, and get everything you can from the feedback. Remember that many professors won't invest that much time or interest."

Tutors

It does not reflect negatively upon you if you decide you would benefit from a tutor; in fact it shows us that you know where your areas of strength are—and are not. Professors expect adult learners to have a level of self-awareness and knowledge of where they need help and then to seek it. Plenty of my older adult students seek out college "kids" to help them with math and even with their writing. If you know where you need to improve and can enlist help, I highly recommend doing so.

Many schools have their own tutoring departments; this may be an advantage of some of the larger educational institutions. If they don't, I would check your local community college or state school. For example, many of my statistics students hire tutors from these sources and they usually prove to be an immense help. Don't be embarrassed or upset if this person is far younger than you. Remember, we all have our strengths and our areas where we could benefit from some assistance. The goal is for you to learn the material in the course, regardless of what additional help it takes.

Getting Help When You Need It

Not only does getting academic assistance help you manage your stress levels, it also allows you to use your limited time to successfully complete course requirements and meet course objectives. Remember, in online universities, we map curriculum in courses to specializations, programs and so on, which is part of the accreditation process. This means that when you do work in one course, in theory it should map to the entire curriculum of the program and the skills you learn in one class will be needed in another class. Truly understanding and grasping the material then becomes most important. Thus, the "method to the madness" : learning the material in one course is truly essential before you move onto the next.

There is, of course, a world of difference between getting help with your writing and having someone write a paper for you. I know this seems obvious, but professors still struggle with this in adult education. Both plagiarism and asking others to write papers (or sharing papers with other students) is unfortunately still common enough that most schools use some form of academic honesty software to detect it. Use these disreputable tactics at great risk to your academic career.

A statistics and research professor at a regionally accredited online institution adds:

"If you cheat, you are cheating yourself.
Do you want your brain surgeon to
have cheated on his medical boards?
Do you want the engineer that
designed the bridge you are driving on
to have cheated his way through his
engineering degree? Remember that
you are in school to learn, not just to

get a piece of paper. I once had a student who wrote his research papers by pulling paragraphs verbatim from website after website and just pasting them into his paper. Needless to say, his papers didn't flow, and they didn't seem to have a thesis. The lack of focus is what prompted me to dig into his paper, and that is how I discovered the plagiarism. I then contacted two of his previous professors, and they found that he had done the same thing on two major papers he had done for them. His profession was in law enforcement!"

If you would like a reference for a tutoring resource, many professors are networked with professors who tutor students, or are aware of other helpful resources. You may also find that your academic adviser is the best person to speak to for advice in finding a tutor or to locate additional academic help if you need it.

Communicating With Your Professor

Be sure you ask any questions you have. When you first enter a class, read the professor's expectations and at least the first week requirements, along with the syllabus. If you have a question, ask! We expect you to; it's our job and if a professor doesn't want to answer questions, it's my view that he or she doesn't belong in the (virtual) classroom. (That doesn't mean you won't run into an unhelpful professor now and again). Remember that there is a real person, committed to academics, on the other side of the keyboard, and the more seriously you treat the academic process, the more you will get out of it.

You will likely run into a professor or two that you just do not like. This isn't any different than what you would encounter in an on ground school. You will find that some grade more strictly on format and writing skills than others; just because one professor didn't point out your double spacing APA issue does not mean that your current professor cannot deduct points for it!

The bottom line is to read and understand all of the course expectations, review all of your professor's feedback before submitting another assignment, and try to remember why you are there when times get tough.

Email

Many professors who teach also travel, or are likely working from a different time zone than you are. When you email your professor, I always recommend that you put the course name and university in the subject line and your specific question in the email. The more information we have right off the bat, the more likely it is we can fully address your question in our first reply, saving you (us) a lot of time and unnecessary back-and-forth messages.

Phone

If your professor is working online, there is a good chance that the listed phone number is his or her personal phone number or cell phone. Just as with email, I always recommend listing the school and course, and your full name and question if you need to leave a voice mail message, along with an email address and a phone number so that we can follow up with you. The more information you leave, the more likely you are to get a thorough response, quickly.

Some professors, like me, use text messaging and instant messaging to take questions from students. This isn't very common yet, and there are some institutions that prohibit it. For example, some schools require that all communication occur only on their servers, email or learning-management systems, for tracking purposes should a dispute arise.

Learning How to Get the Most From Your Professor

There definitely are techniques and best practices you can use to help you get the most out of your relationship with a professor.

First, be very specific with your questions. If it takes an attachment for us to understand where you are stuck—for example, with an equation—I recommend attaching it to the first note. Be candid, and share any concerns you have. If you are afraid of, or intimidated by, a subject, most professors can help put your mind at ease, or at least help you know what to expect. But, if you don't ask, we won't know you need help.

Code of Conduct: What is Acceptable

(And What Might Your Professors Freak Out About)?

Just as with any work situation, professors are employees or contractors of an institution. In online education, we also typically have professional and personal lives to attend to, just like you do. To say we don't have "pet peeves" would just be untrue. It's human nature that if a person is irritated he or she is less likely to be accommodating, so here are some things you may want to know to keep yourself on your professors' good side—and not under his or her skin. Some of the following are my ideas; others have been shared with me by colleagues.

A basic rule of thumb is to approach your professors in the same way you'd like to be approached--respectfully and thoughtfully. Some professors are very concerned with their title being used, so stay on the safe side and assume that they are and address them appropriately.

Students who are dishonest with personal situations or ask for additional time are frustrating and in some cases professors have been known to report them to deans. You know from the beginning of class when the deadlines are, and professors expect you to meet them.

Asking for incompletes at the end of class for a reason other than a health concern or another serious personal issue is frustrating to many professors. Incompletes are not only difficult to track at most universities, but it is unfair for us to grant one learner an incomplete to do work while others are working hard and managing to hold down their personal forts while in school or taking a lower grade – the one they earned. Most of my colleagues will not grant an incomplete unless there is a serious health issue or family loss documented through the advising department.

Trying to get credit for a final project or assignment after a course ends (usually by a day or two and after we already said we do not accept late work) is a pet peeve. Why? Because we have very strict deadlines on when we have to post grades, and we hold your peers accountable to the deadline, too. Do we really want you to drop to a C from an A because you did not submit your final paper? Definitely not, but if we have already submitted grades and previously announced that you must submit your work before the deadline, consider yourself very lucky if you get the grade changed.

Unwarranted appeals are another frustrating issue. Many of us have noticed that the number of grade appeals is going up as education is treated more like a business. If you earned a certain grade, the respectable thing to do is to accept that grade. We will fight grade appeals; if we do not, it implies that we didn't do all we could have to help you, or that our grading was somehow unjust.

Rude and disrespectful "tones" in the online classroom are just as offensive as they would be in person, yet some students (and professors) seem to forget that there is a human on the other side of the keyboard. Remaining respectful in your tone, even if you must clearly express that you disagree with your professor on a given point, will help you successfully get your point across to your professor. And that is the goal after all, right?

Taking What You Learn: Transitioning to Your New Career

After all of your hard work in your on ground or online degree program, you may be itching for a promotion or for a new career altogether. Those of you who wish to teach will take comfort in the wealth of opportunities for online educators and the amount of information available to learn how to break into the world of online education. If you are looking for a promotion, hopefully your managers are impressed by your dedication and investment in yourself, and you have done a good job letting them know about your accomplishments. If you are looking to find another career altogether, you'll certainly have another feather in your cap to move in that direction.

I have been interviewed for dozens of articles on online education and higher education in general, and have been asked thousands of times: "How do students promote themselves and their work to reach the next goal?" Consider all of the things that set you apart as a non-traditional student. First, you invested in yourself. Why should someone else invest in you if you won't do so yourself? Make sure you tell interviewers and people you network with (in a clear, yet tactful way) what you accomplished, and what you sacrificed to do so.

In your resume or curriculum vitae, emphasize the skills you learned through online education that you perhaps would not have in on ground education. For example, you might want to stress the immense writing requirements, even for required course "discussions," which would have been verbal in a traditional environment. Or the amount of time you had to set aside to study. Or the dedication and perseverance it took to juggle the rest of your life with school, and how you set priorities and stuck to them to achieve your ultimate goal. These are intangible traits and skills that virtually any employer will want.

Tangible traits and skills of course include your ability to communicate frequently and succinctly in writing, your ability to network with people you have never met, your ability to work online with different cultures and to network despite the language or culture barrier, and your ability to break down problems into a structured solution model.

If you are on the prowl for an entirely new career, you may want to reach out to fellow alum through the channels your university provides to you. You may wish to join social media groups for former students too, and to continue to be a member of professional communities that will help enhance your growth.

Carissa Pelletier, shared that:

"...many students spend hours writing papers and creating presentations only to forget about them when the term ends. What if all of your hard work could be used beyond just earning a grade? It should be - that's why you went to school!
Employers often conduct an Internet search on candidates as a final step before contacting them for an interview. This technique is generally used to make sure you haven't been posting embarrassing party pictures. Use this opportunity to give them insight into your technical skills and subject knowledge instead. You may want to directly invite employers to your online presence on professional networking sites such as LinkedIn (http://www.linkedin.com/) by including the link on your resume.

Try to stand out from the crowd with a link to an e-portfolio or a dynamic presentation! VisualCV (http://www.visualcv.com/) will create an individual page to highlight your personality and accomplishments. There are also sites such as Carbonmade (http://carbonmade.com/), which is specific to visual fields such as art and design.

Slides from a PowerPoint presentation can be uploaded to a presentation sharing site such as Brainshark: (http://my.brainshark.com). This free site allows you to add audio narration to your slides using a computer microphone or even your cell phone. The site will generate a link to your presentation that you can post on your profile page or include in an email. Imagine employers knowing what your presentations will be like and how dynamic and well written your work is before they even hire you.

Have you ever wondered how websites with tons of content such as eHow, Livestrong and Yahoo! acquire thousands of unique articles and videos? Your technical or creative writing for assignments doesn't have to go to waste after the last day of class. Share your knowledge and possibly be compensated for your work! You can submit original articles, images, videos or slideshows to Yahoo! Contributor Network (http://contributor.yahoo.com/) or apply to be a freelancer for studios such as Demand Media (http://www.demandstudios.com). Some organizations grant continuing education credits for published work. Even if you aren't an English major, freelance work could be a first step in sharpening your writing skills for the future and it looks great on your resume.

Don't be afraid to be the only one you know using these tools. Keep an eye out for unique opportunities within or outside your field. You may find additional tools to stand out from the crowd just waiting to be discovered!"

Terrific advice Carissa! And by now, you are all probably realizing the incredible power of social media for online education – most of the responses and respondents to survey questions came from social media sites!

Emphasize to future employers that you are a believer in lifelong learning, and you don't just walk the walk. You completed your degree and you are bringing invaluable research ability, writing skills and perseverance to your new job.

References

"Blackboard Aims For Standard With Building Blocks Initiative". *Educational Marketer* **31** (33). November 20, 2000.

Blackboard: http://www.blackboard.com

Carnevale, Dan (February 17, 2006). "Justice Department Sees No Antitrust Concerns in Blackboard's Plan to Take Over WebCT". *The Chronicle of Higher Education* **52** (24): p. 37

"Moodle stats page". Moodle.org. http://moodle.org/stats.

The Digital Revolution and Higher Education (2011). Pew Internet & American Life Project. www.pewsocialtrends.org

Publication Manual of the American Psychological Association, Sixth Edition (2012). American Psychological Association, Washington, DC.

Quotes through the text: All quotes are printed with permission from individuals and the social media groups from where they were extracted.

http: turnitin.com (2012).

Index

CPSIA information can be obtained at www.ICGtesting.com
Printed in the USA
LVOW01s1326090715

445604LV00028B/394/P

9 781627 040075